Praise for *A Fable About Mindfulness*

A Gift to Humanity

"The Chaos Antidote is a wonderfully insightful book on the practices of mindfulness. The story allows such inviting descriptions of our everyday life and practical, realistic steps for our own recovery. A gift to humanity."

—**Scott Sweet,** Licensed Clinical Social Worker (LCSW) and Licensed Clinical Addictions Counselor (LCAC)

An Enticing Story

"This is an enticing story, flavored with humor and great insights on mindfulness. It really made me curious to learn more about the topic."

—**Sebastian Seibert,** business management and development leader

A Chaos Antidote

"I was intrigued by the mindfulness tactics in this book. Having a chaotic life myself, they were good reminders to slow down!"

—**Kristen Fuhs Wells,** nonprofit leader and working mother of three

Peaceful Mindfulness Lessons

"This book made me feel like I was there learning mindfulness alongside the characters ... very peaceful and enticing."

—**Andra Kramer,** working mother

An Invitation into the World of Mindfulness

"People both skeptical and curious or eager to learn about mindfulness will find this book inviting and helpful. The Chaos Antidote is a down-to-earth, welcoming, opening-of-a-door invitation for people to step into the world of mindfulness."

—**Nancy Pile,** MAT

THE CHAOS ANTIDOTE

A Fable About Mindfulness

AIMEE L. MORGAN

Copyright © 2020 Aimee Morgan.

All rights reserved. Except as noted, no part of this book may be reproduced, translated, stored in a retrieval system or transmitted, in any form or by any means, electronic, mechanical, photocopying, microfilming, recording or otherwise, without written permission from the Author.

LIMITED PHOTOCOPY LICENSE

The author grants to individual purchasers of this book nonassignable permission to reproduce the GLOWY Daily Reflection Practice. This license is limited to you, the individual purchaser, for personal use.

ISBN: 978-1-7347966-0-5 (Mobi)
978-1-7347966-1-2 (Epub)
978-1-7347966-2-9 (Paperpack)
978-1-7347966-3-6 (Hardback)
978-1-7347966-4-3 (Audiobook)

Library of Congress Control Number: 2020905958

Disclaimer—This is a work of fiction. Names, characters, businesses, places, events, locales and incidents are either the products of the author's imagination or used in a fictitious manner. Any resemblance to actual persons, living or dead, or actual events is purely coincidental.

The information in this volume is not intended as a substitute for consultation with healthcare professionals. Each individual's health concerns should be evaluated by a qualified professional.

Book cover design by Daniel McBride.
Editing by Nancy Pile.
Book interior design & eBook conversion
by Pankaj Runthala at manuscript2ebook.com.
Front cover image by Mika Besfamilnaya.
Author photo by Kayla Harvey.

Published in the United States of America.

First edition publication 2020.
Jade Mermaid Press LLC
P.O. Box 33323
Indianapolis, IN 46203
www.jademermaidpress.com

Dedication

In memory of my father, Tad McBride, who taught me the most mindful lesson of all: how to love with my whole heart

Note that this journey is uniquely yours, no one else's. So the path has to be your own. You cannot imitate somebody else's journey and still be true to yourself. Are you prepared to honor your uniqueness in this way?

—**Jon Kabat-Zinn**

And so may a slow
Wind work these words
Of love around you,
An invisible cloak
To mind your life.

—John O'Donohue, excerpt from poem "Beannacht"

Table of Contents

	A Note Before You Begin	1
Preface:	The Story Behind the Story	3
Chapter 1:	Coffee with Girlfriends	7
Chapter 2:	What Is Mindfulness?	23
Chapter 3:	Week 1: Sitting with Awareness	33
Chapter 4:	Week 2: Awakening the Senses	51
Chapter 5:	Week 3: Mindful Movement	75
Chapter 6:	Week 4: Mindful Creations	101
Chapter 7:	Week 5: Tools to Process Difficult Emotions	127
Chapter 8:	Week 6: Day of Silence	155
Chapter 9:	Six Months Later	175
Appendix A:	Recommended Reading List	185
Appendix B:	Recipe	187
Appendix C:	GLOWY Daily Reflection Practice	191
	Acknowledgments	193
	About the Author	195

A Note Before You Begin

Mindful activities, including mindful movement, can provide great benefits both physically and mentally. But only you know your own body and limits. As with any exercise program, please consult your health care professional with any questions or concerns before starting. When participating in any exercise or exercise program, there is the possibility of physical injury. Not all exercises in this book are suitable for all persons.

The author, its distributors and any other related parties are not liable for any injury, accident or health impairment befalling a reader of this book or any individual utilizing the techniques suggested in this book. The author is not a licensed medical care provider and represents that she has no expertise in diagnosing, examining or treating medical conditions of any kind, or in determining the effect of any specific exercise on a medical condition. The author, its distributors and any other related parties make no representations or warranties with regards to the completeness of information in the book, any linked websites, books or other products represented herein.

If you believe that you may suffer from a physical or emotional impairment, we strongly recommend that you seek advice from a licensed health care professional before embarking on this or any other practice.

The author's goal is to complement self-care by providing information that may encourage healing of the body, mind and spirit. Best results are obtained by exercising common sense and body awareness in the practice of yoga and meditation. To reduce the risk of injury, never force or strain. Supplement your practice with a healthy diet and lifestyle.

Special Note for Women

Pregnant women should not practice any twists or abdominal tightening poses, and should consult with their doctor before beginning any exercise or yoga program. During menses, women should not practice inverted poses, backbends or exercises involving vigorous movements.

Preface
The Story Behind the Story

Ever feel like your world is spinning out of control? That chaos reigns, and you feel helpless to change it?

Not long ago, I found myself in this position, suffering with a blistering intensity. But why? I was married, had two kids, a solid business that I owned, a nice home in a thriving urban neighborhood. I seemed to have all the things.

And yet I was unhappy. So unhappy.

I frantically distracted myself, constantly reaching for my phone, a shopping cart, a work file. Yet nothing satisfied me. The more I ran from my discomfort, the more I needed to run. Anxiety plagued me.

Exhaustion set in as I realized a humbling truth: I didn't like who I'd become—someone who relied upon other people and things to satisfy me and validate my worth. I experienced a crisis of faith, finally acknowledging my heartache from personal and professional relationships.

I saw two choices: Continue to run and suffer *or* find another way.

I chose another way.

I sought to discover why I was miserable. I buried myself in self-help books, attended classes and trainings, collected inspirational quotes. I tried to do all the things.

Years of studying psychology, relationship and spiritual tomes unearthed bits of wisdom. However, one day I stepped back and discovered that my voracious pursuit of knowledge had led me to an unexpected path: the path of mindfulness.

I balked at first. How could sitting, walking, moving and eating with undivided attention fix anybody's problems?

While I've written this book about mindfulness, I didn't grow up all "namaste." I grew up in a small Indiana farming community. I come from a long line of farmers and construction workers—firmly established in the Bible Belt of America.

Logically, I was skeptical about mindfulness. I kept expecting it to get weird. That people would start talking about the "Universe." That my friends would start staring at me wide-eyed and speechless as I explained how I sat on a cushion to calm myself. I wondered: Is this another religion that I'm not comfortable with? What will I have to give up or give into to achieve a reasonable level of mastery?

Despite my skepticism, I chose to trust where I was being led. I took the Mindfulness-Based Stress Reduction course developed by Jon Kabat-Zinn, an eight-week course that helps participants learn how to be mindful. I faithfully practiced sitting quietly, moving attentively and creating thoughtfully, showing up for life—even when I felt like I would crawl out of my skin from the desire to run away. I felt a profound shift in my thoughts, feelings, body and energy as I learned to *just be, just notice, just breathe*.

Amidst the trial and error of healing and learning, I opened my heart to many women and heard their stories of struggle: loss of direction, chronic anxiety, physical suffering and haunting pasts. I felt called to write a parable to help equip others with the knowledge and skills to ease their suffering and find lasting peace and joy inside themselves.

Sure, folks from some locations or communities may be reading this and thinking, "Mindfulness isn't anything new."

True. However, if you're from a place where mindfulness is mainstream, sometimes it's worth revisiting. What does mindfulness really mean? Even if it's normalized, are you practicing it in today's electronica? What could it do for you if you practiced it faithfully?

Now, I'm not a monk writing from a mountainside retreat. I'm not an ordained minister of any type. I'm not even a certified yoga instructor. But I'm a woman/wife/mother/business owner who's faced pain and found a more fulfilling and joyful way of living for myself. I developed a daily practice that includes GLOWY, an original daily reflection practice that I created and will share with you in this book. I found an antidote to chaos.

The antidote to chaos: mindfulness.

I discovered that all healing—and power—comes from being fully present in each moment. My experience taught me that the only way to heal is to sit with pain, look it in the face and feel it move through yourself as you breathe deeply. Then you can accept pain for what it is: a perfect teacher.

The lessons in this book transformed my life. This book, a realistic yet fictional story, follows the tale of a small group of women who experience mindfulness training firsthand and personally experience its life-changing—and life-giving power. But this book isn't just for women—it's for anyone who's looking for an antidote to chaos.

It's my sincere hope that the journey of the women in this story inspires and empowers you. May your life shine, illuminating the path for others, as you harness the power of ancient wisdom to combat modern stress.

If you'd like to learn more about mindfulness beyond the lessons in this book, I invite you to visit **aimeemorgan.com**. Here you'll find further resources—including a free six-week mindfulness guide—and ways to connect.

Chapter 1
Coffee with Girlfriends

When we get too caught up in the busyness of the world, we lose connection with one another—and ourselves.

—Jack Kornfield

"Sorry I'm late," I said. "I only have fifteen minutes, but I really wanted to see you two."

The roar of the quirky coffee shop seemed to dull for a moment.

"Fifteen minutes?" Simone replied, slinging her oversized pink purse onto her shoulder and hugging me. "Meghan, we have some major catching up to do."

I glanced at the counter, decorated with local concert posters and poetry reading events.

"I'll have a cappuccino, please," I said to the barista, pushing my red braid over my shoulder. "The kids have swimming club."

The barista, a bohemian guy with blonde dreads, smiled at me.

"Meghan, is there any way Pat could help this afternoon?" Lucia asked, reaching up to grab her hug. "That way we could get more time with you."

"My hubby is showing a property to a potential investor," I replied, wiping imaginary sweat from my forehead. "How are you two? Any international service trips planned soon, Lucia?"

"I'd love to return to Sierra Leone, like the trip you featured in your article years ago," Lucia said. "But no, no trips planned at this time."

"That article was my favorite piece," I said. "Writing that was one of the most rewarding experiences of my life."

"Was that the article that won you that fancy award?" Simone asked, adjusting the collar on my white button-up shirt. "The one about the interfaith mission trip led by your dad, Lucia and her fiancé?"

"Yeah," I said, pulling down on the bottom of my vest.

"Former fiancé," Lucia said, looking at the ground, her glossy black hair falling forward.

"Sorry to bring up old business, Lucy Lou," Simone said. "I'm never sure what to call him."

"It's fine," Lucia said, pushing back the cuticles on her light brown fingers.

"I'm busy," Simone said, pushing back a curl of her unruly black hair from her dark brown face. "Looking for a new job."

"What?" Lucia said, pulling her cardigan together. "I thought your job was secure."

"I thought so, too," Simone said, flashing her bright pink gel nails as she shrugged. "I've worked at the same nonprofit for five years. Funding was cut for my position, so I'm currently unemployed."

"What are you going to do?" I asked.

"I've got some leads," she said. "I'm trying not to freak out about paying my mortgage next month."

"How are you making ends meet?" Lucia asked.

"A little bit of savings that should last me a month, maybe two," Simone said. "I'm a single woman and at real risk of moving myself and my kids back in with my mom. But enough about me, let's get the scoop on Miss I've-Got-to-Leave-in-Fifteen-Minutes."

I forcefully blew back my long bangs as I looked down at my cell phone.

"My girls are busy with soccer, swimming and music lessons," I said. "Pat's business is going well, and I'm … well, I'm at a crossroads, kind of like Simone."

"Do tell," Simone said, handing me my cappuccino and grabbing the other two coffees.

Simone chose a small table in a quiet corner. As we sat down, I bit my lower lip.

"It's early in our conversation today for sharing this," I said. "But time is short and Brené Brown would tell me to suck it up and get vulnerable, so here goes."

I took a big swig of the cappuccino.

Is this a good idea? I haven't told anyone, even Pat, what's going on with me. Just blurt it out, Meg.

"I am so unhappy and empty that I'm scared what I might do," I said, biting my thumbnail. "I've thought about establishing my freelance writing as a business or going back to get my master's. But I'm utterly frazzled with taking care of the kids and supporting Pat's business."

Lucia and Simone nodded. I placed my left hand behind my stiff neck.

"I kind of feel dead inside," I said. "Like nothing satisfies me, and I'm not even sure who I am anymore."

"Whoa, girl," Simone said. "That's exactly what you said to me several years ago. Are we on the brink of a Double-O Seven Mystery of the Missing Meg sequel?"

"I missed something," Lucia said. "What was the Double-O Seven Mystery?"

"Don't you remember?" Simone said. "In 2007, two double-O seven, the year before Meg's twins were born, she disappeared for a week without a word to anyone. We dubbed it the Double-O Seven Mystery of the Missing Meg and hoped that the greatest Hollywood sin, a bad sequel, would never surface."

"Ah, yes, I remember," Lucia said. "I'd just forgotten the nickname."

"I don't know," I said, rubbing my neck. "That time I was just overwhelmed and uncertain about my future."

"And how is that different than now?" Simone asked. "Other than the fact that I'm assuming you don't have tickets to an African safari in your purse this time. You don't, do you?"

I pursed my lips, knowing what *was* in my purse.

"No," I said, shaking my head.

"Listen, girl," Simone said. "You have two kids now who are relying on you."

I nodded slowly.

"Focus on what you're good at, like writing," Simone said. "You always figure it out, even if it's a royal pain. And if all else fails, I hear Bali is gorgeous this time of year."

I checked my phone again.

"Ugh. Speaking of pain. Pat just texted," I said. "He's going to be super late for dinner. Again."

Tears welled in my eyes.

"It's a miracle if we have dinner as a family," I said. "And even if we do, everyone's on their phones. It never feels like we're really together anymore."

Simone handed me a tissue while Lucia put her hand on mine.

"I don't want to ruin everything," I said. "But I don't know if I can keep going on like this."

The coffee shop bell rang as *she* stepped in. The three of us looked up to see her radiant olive-skin face, framed with wavy white-and-gray hair that flowed to her mid-back.

"Who is *that*?" Simone asked, eyebrows raised.

"That's Veda, the mother of mindfulness," Lucia said. "She's my hero."

"How do you know her?" Simone asked.

"My mother went to college with her," Lucia said. "Mama and Veda are dear friends. She's my godmother."

"Wait, I thought Meg's dad was your godfather," Simone said.

"Yeah, he is," Lucia said. "Godparents aren't always married."

Simone gave her a thumbs-up in understanding.

"*Hola*, Lucia," Veda said, opening her arms wide for a hug.

After a long embrace, Lucia introduced Veda to us.

"It's a pleasure to meet you ladies," Veda said.

"Would you join us?" Lucia asked, smoothing her khakis and sitting down.

"I'd be honored to join you, but please allow me to get some tea first," Veda said. "It warms my heart … and my bones."

I checked my phone again. When I looked up, I met Simone's convicting eyes.

"I'm sorry," I said. "I'll put this away."

"Good," Simone said. "Your hair is lovely, but I want to see more than the top of your ginger locks."

With a lopsided grin, I slid my phone into my purse.

"I feel like I've seen Veda before," Simone said.

"She's Cora's sister," Lucia said. "That's how I connected with Cora's daycare for my niece Adriana."

"Wait, she's Cora's sister?" Simone asked. "Maybe that's where I've seen her while dropping off my kiddos at Cora's."

"I've heard Cora talk about all the fun she has visiting her sister out of state," I said. "They look a lot alike."

"That's because they're twins," Lucia said.

Veda slowly pulled out a chair and sat down beside Lucia. She took a long look across the table at me. I felt like she could see something in me that I couldn't. I felt a twinge to check my phone.

With both hands cupped around her steaming mug of tea, Veda lifted the cup to her nose, closed her eyes and took a long breath in and out.

"Would you ladies like to smell my tea?" Veda asked.

We stared at her, wide-eyed.

"Sure," Lucia offered, taking a sniff over Veda's cup. "Smells very earthy, like seaweed or warm wheat bread."

"Mmmm, black Pu-erh tea, one of my favorites," Veda said, adjusting her red flowing scarf. "I'm feeling a bit rushed, so I'm going to take three deep breaths. Feel free to join me."

We watched her take the first two breaths, then joined in on the last breath.

"Ah, much better," Veda said, smiling, then sipping her tea.

"What did you call that tea?" Simone asked.

"Pu-erh, sounds like POO-air," Veda said.

"Yeah, that's what I thought you said."

"Did you decide if you're staying in town?" Lucia asked. "Mama told me you're renting a place."

"I'm back in town for the spring and summer to teach a few college classes," she replied. "We're renting a home on the east side, Garrett's old house, actually, and thinking about moving back. My son wanted me to tell you hello."

Lucia pursed her lips.

"Is it still standing?" Lucia asked.

Veda nodded.

"Who's Garrett?" Simone asked.

"He's …" Lucia began.

"He's my brother-in-law," Veda said. "My husband's younger brother."

Veda took a sip of her tea, eyeing Lucia.

"Did you tell your friends that I'm a deep breather?" Veda asked.

I laughed awkwardly, looking at Lucia for direction. She stared at Veda for a few beats too long.

Simone and I raised an eyebrow at each other.

"I told them you are the mother of mindfulness," Lucia said.

"That's very generous of you," Veda said, smiling broadly.

"Simone and Meghan have taken their children to Cora's daycare since their kids were infants, just like Adriana," Lucia said.

"Did you meet through Cora?" Veda asked.

"Actually we three go way back," Lucia said. "Meg's father is my godfather, as you know."

"Yeah, Lucia was like a surrogate sister," I said. "She was always at my house growing up. Simone and I met at college. Our boyfriends, who we eventually married, were best friends. Kinda still are. It's complicated. Anyway, fast-forward a few years, Simone and I have a couple kids apiece."

"Now our kiddos are great friends, too," Simone said. "Cookouts, campouts, hideouts, you name it. Our kids are always looking for excuses to hang out. So are Pat and Anthony, even though Anthony and I aren't together anymore."

"Adriana goes to the same school as Meghan and Simone's kids," Lucia said.

"Now that they're graduated from Cora's," I said with a pouty face. "Lucia's the one who introduced us to your sister."

"My sister is a beautiful, generous person," Veda said. "I'm so blessed to have her in my life, as I'm sure you all are, too."

"She's been like a second mom to my kids," I said. "She's enabled me to grow my freelance business and has treated us like family."

"That's a wonderful thing to hear," Veda said. "Now that I know how we're all connected, I'm interested in your stories. Would you tell me a little more about yourselves?"

"I run, um, *ran* a local nonprofit that serves kids," Simone said. "Looking for a new job. I have two kids, a boy and a girl. I'm a single mom and not looking for any matchmaking assistance."

Simone shot me a look with pursed lips.

"I'm a freelance writer," I said. "Married to a real-estate developer and am the mother of twin girls."

I showed her a photo of the twins on my phone.

"They have your beautiful red hair," Veda said.

"And you know me," Lucia said.

"Indeed I do, Lucia," Veda said. "A thoughtful woman and bright engineer. How's work? You're still at the large firm downtown, right? And how's your … your niece?"

"Adriana is doing well," Lucia said, showing Veda her phone's screensaver, a close-up of Adriana. "She's eight years old now."

"Adriana has always had such stunning hazel eyes," Veda said. "Just like her father's."

Lucia's glistening eyes locked with Veda's while I took a long drag of my coffee.

Is it just me or is there something going on that I don't know about?

"Umm, did I miss something?" Simone asked, staring over her cup at Lucia.

Lucia cleared her throat.

"Yes, I love Adriana's eyes," Lucia said. "And, yes, I'm still working downtown and enjoying it."

"That's wonderful." Veda said. "It's a blessing to love one's work."

"It is, and I do feel blessed," Lucia said quietly.

Lucia placed her right hand across her chest as she looked down for a few moments. She took a deep breath in and blew it out forcefully.

"However, the real reason I invited everyone today was to tell you some difficult news," Lucia said, placing her left hand over her right hand, as if trying to hold her heart in. She rubbed her prayer bead bracelet with her thumb, the glass mustard seed bulb empty as always.

My stomach flipped. We gazed at her quietly with concerned eyes.

"Remember the last time we were scheduled to get together, and I bailed at the last minute?" Lucia asked.

Simone and I nodded.

"I had just returned from the doctor," Lucia said. "And I couldn't bring myself to talk about it."

"To talk about what?" I asked.

"I've been diagnosed with cancer," Lucia said. She pursed her lips and scanned our faces.

"Oh, Lucia!" Simone said, throwing her arms around Lucia.

Veda and I joined, wrapping Lucia in a large, layered human hug.

After unfurling from our hug, we sat in silence, looking pensively at Lucia.

"What type of cancer is it?" I asked. "When were you diagnosed? What stage are you in?"

"Easy, detective Meg," Simone said. "Give her a moment to breathe."

"I was diagnosed about a month ago but wanted a second opinion," Lucia said. "This week I received confirmation from the second doctor that I have stage four breast cancer."

I stopped breathing.

"The doctor told me it is terminal."

"I don't understand," Simone said. "You're so young. You've got to be at least six or seven years younger than me. What, twenty-eight?"

"I'm twenty-nine," Lucia said. "He said that cancer is rarer for Latinas. But when it strikes, it can progress quickly and be more difficult to treat."

"Stage four means it has spread, right?" Simone asked.

"It has spread to my bones," Lucia said. "I'd been seeing my doctor for nagging hip and back pain. I thought it was from pulling long hours at the office."

She took a sip of coffee, then a deep breath.

"After many months of physical therapy and other treatments, my doctor ordered an X-ray and MRI. The MRI showed a two-centimeter lump in my breast, which spread to my hips and lower back. My doctor thinks it's been growing aggressively for the last two or three years. The good news is that it's possible to live up to ten years with treatment."

"Have you told your family?" I asked. "Have you told my dad?"

"I'm planning to tell them soon," Lucia said. "I'm just not sure how or when to do it."

"How are you feeling, physically?" Veda asked, placing her veined hand on Lucia's forearm.

"I'm OK, considering I just started chemo," Lucia said. "The vomiting and exhaustion get to me, so most days I sneak off to my car to take a nap. I also am losing feeling in my hands and feet. The doctor said neuropathy is normal."

"And how are you feeling emotionally?" Veda asked.

Lucia took a deep breath as she ran her fingers through the sides of her shiny shoulder-length black hair. Upon pulling her hands away, she stared down at her hand. A clump of hair was woven through her fingers.

"Most of my life I've kept my head down and worked hard," Lucia said. "I never really thought much about my feelings. But I sense strongly that I need to slow down and listen to my body."

"Sometimes our body tells us something our heart needs to hear," said Veda. "Would you be open to learning how to do that?"

"Learning to do what?" Lucia asked.

"Slow down and listen to yourself, your body, mind and spirit."

"*Absolutamente*," Lucia said. "What do you recommend?"

"The universe has impeccable timing. I'm leading a mindfulness introduction session at the university tomorrow at noon," Veda said, slowly sipping her tea. "Would you join me?"

"I'll be there," Lucia said.

How on earth is a mindfulness session going to help Lucia? Seems like we're adding one more thing to her full plate. Doesn't she just need to rest?

"Well, if you're going, I am, too," Simone said. "Lucia, you're not doing this alone. If you're going, we are, too. Right, Meghan?"

"Mindfulness, as in a woo-woo practice?" I asked, folding my arms across my chest.

"Woo-woo?" Simone asked.

"Yeah, like New-Agey mumbo jumbo." I said. "Look, I'm a believer, a preacher's daughter. I want to support you, Lucia, in all this chaos. But I need assurance that things won't get all weird and mystical."

"Meghan," Veda said. "My journey has taught me that very few things in life provide assurance. I invite you to give the session a try and see what you think."

With a tilted head I checked my calendar, grimacing as I scanned several appointments I'd need to reschedule.

"OK, this is for Lucia," I said. "I'll be there, too. Tomorrow only, though."

Tears filled Lucia's dark brown eyes and her chin quivered.

"Beautiful," Veda said, placing her hand on Lucia's forearm. "I invite you to do one thing before you attend."

My phone's alarm sounded, indicating it was time for me to leave. Simone's eyes darted to my face, and I silenced my phone.

"What's that?" Simone asked Veda.

"Breathe deeply for one minute and focus only on your breath, noticing how it feels going in and out of your body," Veda said. "I also encourage you, Meghan and Simone, to consider how mindfulness, being fully present, might serve you."

Simone and I nodded.

"I feel honored by what you each have shared," Veda said. "I will keep you in my heart as I travel through my day."

"Thank you for listening and inviting us to your class tomorrow," Lucia said.

"It's my pleasure," Veda said. "Now I must bid you farewell, so I can teach my afternoon class. I look forward to seeing you three tomorrow. Oh, and lunch will be provided."

Veda rose from her seat.

"Lucia, may I hug you again?" Veda asked.

Lucia stood and wrapped her arms under Veda's arms and laid her head on Veda's chest. They hugged for a full minute before Lucia let go.

"You give the best hugs," Lucia said.

"You want to know the secret to my hugs?" Veda asked.

Lucia nodded.

"I always hold on, never letting go until the other person is ready to release our hug," Veda said. "Silently I reflect on my gratefulness for the person in my arms."

She bowed to each of us. Haphazardly, we each nodded to her. We looked at each other with gentle grins and tilted heads. The coffee shop bell rang again, signaling her departure.

"No one has ever bowed to me before," Simone said.

"Me neither," I said. "She's an intriguing woman."

"You have no idea," Lucia said.

Chapter 2
What Is Mindfulness?

Mindfulness means paying attention in a particular way on purpose, in the present moment non-judgmentally.

—Jon Kabat-Zinn

"Welcome," Veda said, bowing to us at the door of the university's writing center, a large and stately brick building.

"Please have a seat in our circle, we are about to begin," Veda said to the ten guests chatting in clusters throughout the room.

A smattering of mismatched armchairs formed two U-shaped rows radiating from the front where Veda stood. The cozy room, filled with books and sunlight, made me ache for a journal and pen.

As I sat next to Lucia, I caught a whiff of vomit.

Oh, mercy, poor Lucia's been sick today.

"Thank you for joining me for Mindfulness Matters," Veda began. "Today I'll provide an introduction to mindfulness. I'll also share with you the legendary tale of Queen Alba. And we'll conclude with time for questions and answers."

The door opened and Simone rushed to scooch between me and Lucia. She wore what looked like a brand-new navy-blue knee-length dress with matching pumps.

How can she afford a snazzy new outfit with her mortgage in jeopardy? Calm down, Meg. Maybe she has an interview today.

"Does anyone know what mindfulness is?" Veda asked.

"Sporting a well-paired outfit," Simone whispered in my ear. "What is that awful smell?"

I darted my eyes from Simone to Lucia and back to Simone in a tense response. Simone covered her mouth in a silent gasp. She offered Lucia a mint.

"Paying attention," a young man said.

"Yes," Veda said. "Paying attention to what?"

Answers popped around the room: "Ourselves." "Other people." "Nature."

"You are a smart group of people," Veda said. "Mindfulness is paying attention to what's going on inside and around us. Our breath is the bridge between the two. Noticing where we are and what we're thinking or feeling without reacting to it."

She moved across the front of the room.

"Did you know whenever you practice awareness, noticing your thoughts, feelings and sensations, you're being mindful? So you can practice anytime and anyplace. I call it 'being with what is.'

"We cultivate the capacity to be mindful through practicing meditation. Or, intentionally being with what is.

"I invite you to close your eyes. Take three deep breaths with me, focusing on your breath traveling in and out."

Oh, boy, here we go.

"Breathing in, notice the sensations your in-breath has," Veda said. "Breathing out, notice the sensations your out-breath has.

"Now you may open your eyes. What did you notice?"

"I felt the hot air from the register blowing on my face," said Simone.

"You noted a physical sensation," Veda said.

"I was thinking about all the things I have to get done this afternoon," I said.

"You noticed a thought, or a series of thoughts," Veda said.

"I felt uneasiness about my life, yet gratefulness for the support of my friends," Lucia said.

Simone put her arm around Lucia's shoulders. I noticed Lucia wince.

"That's an awareness of your feelings," Veda said. "In mindfulness, we notice what comes up and try to replace judgment with curiosity. So, when we feel ourselves getting carried away by our thoughts or a to-do list, we can step back and say, 'Isn't that interesting that in a moment of quiet I thought of laundry, conflict or illness?'

"As I mentioned at the beginning, mindfulness is developed through meditation. Meditation is simply breathing, quieting our minds, practicing being present with our breath, so we can be present for other important parts of our lives—our thoughts, feelings and physical sensations, as well as our relationships and work. It's a powerful practice and has the ability to rewire the structure of your brain."

"How long does it take to cultivate mindfulness?" a woman asked.

"You may have grown up playing basketball. Did you go from holding a basketball for the first time to scoring the winning basket in the same day? Probably not. You learned to bounce that air-filled, orange-brown sphere. Up and down, like an in-and-out breath. You built upon that dribbling skill to be able to pass the ball. Then shoot the ball. But you'd never be ready to play a game of basketball if you hadn't learned the basic principle of up-and-down dribbling, right?

"The same goes for meditation, or mindful breathing. If you can master the skill of breathing mindfully in and out, you will be equipped to develop mindful skills in other areas of life, like fully listening in a business meeting, staying present during a difficult conversation with a loved one or giving thoughtful space to your own joys and wounds. Even paying attention to your own physical discomfort."

Veda paused and looked at Lucia for a moment.

Lucia whispered something to Simone, and she removed her arm from Lucia's shoulders.

"Now I want to tell you a story that has nothing to do with basketball, but everything to do with mindfulness. It's the story of Queen Alba and the Lynx, one of my favorite tales that my mother would tell me as a child."

In the land of Lavandula reigned the wise Queen Alba. She loved her people, including her precious young niece, Mara.

At the kingdom's annual Lavender Festival the queen and many of her kinsmen became entranced with small blue mirrors for sale. Everyone wanted one of their own and became dazed by its power of escape. The blue mirrors offered mesmerizing photos and stories from far-off places. Within a few hours the citizens knew more about people they'd never met than their own neighbors.

The kingdom fell into a trance, everyone distracted by their blue mirrors. One day, a coachman driving Mara, the queen's niece, became bored and pulled out his blue mirror for distraction. He failed to notice that he was driving dangerously close to the edge of the cliff. He faltered, sending both himself and the queen's niece down the cliff to their deaths.

In her grief, the queen walked at length into the woods. She came across a cottage. An old woman with radiant blue eyes greeted her and introduced her to Link, a breathtaking lynx with spotted brown fur and honey brown eyes.

Queen Alba was a bit fearful of Link. The old woman explained that while the lynx could be dangerous, it was the queen's job to train her. The old woman instructed the queen to walk Link to the aspen tree in the field, some distance away, staying present with her breath and footsteps. She warned her of the dust and to avoid engaging in conflict with the lynx.

The queen, impatient to complete the task, ran toward the tree. But the faster she ran, the farther away the tree became. Link took her cue and ran away from the queen.

Defeated, yet finally reunited with Link, Queen Alba returned to the old woman's house. As she grieved about the past and worried about the future, Link walked in circles, creating a dust storm. Queen Alba struggled to breathe.

The old woman said the lynx was prone to running away and pacing with worry.

Day after day the queen attempted to reach the golden tree in the field. But she was consumed by her troubling thoughts. The lynx kept running from her and circling her, making dust fly.

One day Queen Alba had enough. She became angry at Link for her disobedience. Her yelling caused Link to claw the ground with her paw. In her fear the queen stepped away from Link and fell off the cliff into the sea below.

The queen awoke on the shore, with Link licking her face. Link had saved her!

The queen removed Link's chain, and they walked to the aspen tree slowly, silently and with great awareness. The two were in perfect tune with one another.

After a peaceful night's sleep, the queen awoke to find that Link was gone.

She knocked on the old woman's door to tell her the disturbing news. But the old woman was not old anymore. She was a beautiful young maiden with the old woman's radiant blue eyes.

When the queen told her Link was missing, she responded, "That's good. The lynx now lives inside you, dear one. You are free to go."

Then she opened the door of her house to reveal dozens of lynxes.

Before departing the queen made a request.

At the doorway to her kingdom, the queen shouted to the guardsmen: "Fling wide the gates!"

As they did, she took a deep breath and looked back to see the group of lynxes behind her. They followed her through the open gates and into the kingdom of Lavandula.

Veda stayed quiet for several moments.

"What do you make of this story?" she asked.

What Is Mindfulness?

"Distractions are things that keep us from being present with our true nature," I said. "When we lose touch with ourselves and others, tragic consequences can result."

"But facing our situation—both inside and out—with mindful breath and awareness is the key to returning to ourselves," said Lucia.

"Beautifully said, ladies," Veda said.

"As we transition to our next interaction, please quietly get your plate of salad from the table, and return to your seat," she said. "As you eat, please remain quiet and notice the flavors in your salad."

After lunch and Q&As the mindfulness session came to an end. Before departing, Lucia, Simone and I gathered around Veda.

"Do you have more of those mints, Simone?" Lucia asked.

Simone handed her the roll. "Just keep them."

"How can we learn more and practice what you've taught us, Veda?" Lucia asked, plopping down on a chair with exhaustion.

"After our discussion at the coffee shop yesterday, I began thinking about how I might help you three while trying out a new course I want to pitch to the university," Veda said. "I'd like to lead you in a private six-week class, just the three of you."

I rustled in my purse, feeling for my phone. Four missed calls and five missed texts.

I need to make this quick and get back to work.

"When do we start?" Simone asked. "I'm in a tough situation and could use all the help I can get. I mean, I love my mom but don't want to be roomies again."

"Meghan, how are you feeling after today's session?" Veda asked. "Is mindfulness something you'd be open to exploring?"

My phone vibrated. I blew out a loud breath.

"I'm not sure, ladies," I said, shaking my head.

Lucia got up from the couch and stood in front of me, eyes pleading. With half a foot of height on her, I could see a bald spot on the top of her head. Tears beaded in my eyes.

Lucia, my surrogate sister, is dying.

I crossed my arms, looking at Lucia, then Veda. "You promise no woo-woo?"

"Remember what Veda said," Simone said. "Life has no assurances, only opportunities to explore."

"This is for Lucia," I said.

"And who knows, Miss No-Woo-Woo may have a few life issues to work on herself," Simone said.

"Like what?" I asked.

"Let's see," Simone said. "Like avoiding the Double-O Seven sequel?"

"How about this weekend?" Lucia asked.

I cringed, thinking about all the favors I'd need to ask to make this weekend happen—babysitter, meals, schlepping kids to and from practice. Grabbing my phone, I scrolled through my calendar.

"I can do that," said Veda. "You are invited to my home for the next six Saturday mornings, starting at 7 a.m. Just let me know by Friday if you can commit to it. The course will be challenging, but deeply rewarding."

"Deal," Simone and Lucia said in unison.

"I'll do my best to make it happen," I said, looking up from my phone.

"Excellent," Veda said. "Oh, and what are your favorite colors?"

"Hello?"

"Hi, Dad," I said.

"Hey, honey."

"Is it a good time to chat?" I asked.

"I'm leading a mission training session here at the church, but the team is taking a break," he said. "I have a few minutes. What's going on?"

"You know Veda?"

"Of course."

"She's asked me, Lucia and Simone to join her for a six-week mindfulness course she's leading," I said. "Just the three of us."

"OK," he said, rustling some papers. "And … you're unsure about it?"

"I'm wondering what you think about Veda," I said. "I love Lucia like a sister, but I'm not sure this course is a good fit."

He exhaled loudly.

"Twenty-five, thirty years ago, when Lucia's mom asked me to be Lucia's godfather and Veda to be her godmother, I was flabbergasted," he said. "I pushed back. I mean, I was a ministry leader and Veda, well, she was some hippy crackpot as far as I was concerned."

"And is she?"

"A hippy crackpot?" he asked. "No. Veda is Veda."

"What does that mean?" I asked.

"It means Veda has taught me so much, sweetheart," he said. "I said some harsh, judgmental things about Veda in the past, while you were growing up."

"Like 'she's a hippy crackpot,'" I said.

"Yes," he said. "I used to be consumed by the rules, not love. But not Veda. People always come first in her book. She's always chosen love."

"That's great, but I'm still not sure if I should take the course."

"Look, Meg, nothing in life is certain," he said. "Hold on just a sec."

I heard mumblings of a crowd.

"Training resumes in two minutes," he announced loudly.

"Like I was saying, nothing is certain," he said. "And Lucia needs you more than ever."

"Wait, Lucia told you about … "

"Yes," he said, his voice cracking. "If you're looking for my support, you have it. And you never know what Veda's teachings might have in store for you."

"Thanks, Dad."

"You're welcome. I love you, Meg. I've got to run, but let me know what you decide."

Chapter 3
Week 1: Sitting with Awareness

*If you want to conquer the anxiety of life,
live in the moment, live in the breath.*

—Amit Ray

As we entered Veda's home, I smelled something sweet.

"Good morning, Veda," I said. "What's that lovely smell?"

"Palo santo," she replied. "It's my favorite scent, so calming, warm and beautiful. Like gathering around a campfire with dear friends."

"Well, it's delicious," said Simone. "It's got me craving s'mores."

Simone and I sat on Veda's couch. I felt my cross necklace smack down on my chest.

Relax, Meg. Lucia needs you.

Lucia stood just inside the doorway, pushing back her cuticles and looking around the room like she was entering a haunted house. Veda hugged her.

"You told me we'd meet at Garrett's old house, but I can't quite believe it," Lucia said. "It feels surreal to be here."

"I hope it's not too much for you to handle," Veda whispered.

Simone and I gave each other a raised eyebrow.

Veda sat opposite us in a burgundy upholstered armchair.

"Meghan, Simone, Lucia, I'm truly honored you've joined me today," Veda said. "The sun is shining and I feel warmth in my spirit as I behold your faces. I know we are gathering in the midst of difficult news of Lucia's health. I ask that you be present with the thoughts and sensations you feel around this, as well as what comes up naturally around your own lives."

She paused, looking each of us in the eye, one by one. Smiling and slowly bowing from her seat, her deep red glass-beaded earrings falling forward.

"I ask you to join me in a screen-free time today," Veda said. "Please silence your phones."

All three of us scrounged for our phones and turned off the sound.

First Check-In

"Let's begin by checking in with ourselves," Veda said. "Please close your eyes and breathe in fully. Now breathe out fully. Continue breathing for the next minute."

After our minute breathing exercise, we looked up at her.

"What did you notice?" she asked.

"I'm tired," said Simone. "It's 7 a.m. on a Saturday, and I've already dropped off the kids at Anthony's, my ex."

WEEK 1: SITTING WITH AWARENESS

"I'm also tired, for different reasons," said Lucia. "I'm trying to stay strong for my family and job, but I'm overwhelmed, not knowing what will happen to me."

"I kept smelling the palo santo," I said. "It reminds me of summer camp."

"Once again you ladies have captured the basic nature of meditation: Noticing what's inside and around us and maintaining a sense of curiosity. Being aware of our thoughts: 'I'm tired.' Paying attention to our senses by smelling the palo santo. Noticing our feelings, like anxiety.

"We can be quick to justify, judge and join our experiences. I'm tired—*thought*—because it's early—*justifying*. I am sad—*emotion*—because I need to stay strong—*judge*. I smell a scent—*sense*— and I am connecting it to summer camp—*join*.

"It's natural to connect dots through justifying, judging and joining. Our brain's job is to think, always looking for past experiences to justify a response, judge what we should do or join a train of thought. But these reactions can remove us from our current experiences.

"We are invited to just notice our experiences—both internally and externally. We may still think the same thoughts, but instead of grabbing hold of them, naming them as good or bad, we let them pass and take the 'Isn't that interesting … ?' approach.

"So, Simone, you had the thought, 'I'm tired.' And that you're tired because it's early and you dropped the kids off already this morning. Think about how loving it is to realize you had the two separate thoughts: 'I'm tired' and 'It's because it's 7 a.m. and I've had a lot to do already.' And to think, 'Isn't that interesting that I sense that I'm tired? Isn't it also interesting that I connect my tiredness to the time and activities of the morning?'

"Meditation is about noticing what's inside and around us while remaining nonjudgmental, curious, loving and kind toward ourselves. And our breath grounds us, helping us practice presence in a small, tangible way that's always available to us. Breathing is the basis of all our mindfulness practice."

Noticing Our Surroundings

"Please take the next two minutes and notice what's around you, without judgment and only curiosity."

I smelled a manly scent lingering.

"Besides the palo santo, I notice a hint of Brut cologne," I said. "My dad always wore Brut … oops, I joined again. I notice Brut in the air."

"I also smell the same scent," said Veda. "My husband has worn Brut since we first met."

"I saw your red earrings sparkling in the light," said Simone.

"I heard a cardinal chirping outside," said Lucia.

"I felt the smooth fabric of my chair," said Veda.

Tea Time

"I now want us to try out the final sense: taste. Please join me in silence while we make a pot of tea, so we can enjoy all our senses: we can see, smell, touch, taste and hear the glory of this tea. Lucia, would you make the tea for us while we join you in the kitchen?"

"Sure thing," said Lucia. "Do you still use that old kettle to brew the tea?"

In silence, we followed her. As Lucia filled the metal kettle with water, it sounded like she was spraying the inside of a steel drum. She placed the kettle on the gas stovetop.

Tick, tick, tick, whoosh went the burner, flaming vibrant blue then fervent orange.

Veda invited us to smell the loose-leaf tea. The minutes passed before we heard a rumble in the kettle, then a soft whistle followed by a loud whistle. We watched as Lucia turned off the burner. She poured the steaming water into the ceramic kettle, over the mound of loose-leaf tea, and closed the circular metal lid with a *tink*. Veda placed four ceramic mugs on the countertop.

Five minutes later, Lucia poured the light yellow liquid into our mugs. She passed us the mugs. Instantly I felt the warmth on my hands. After a few quiet moments, Veda lifted the mug to her nose and took a long inhale. We followed her lead.

I saw Lucia gag a bit on the smell.

We all took a sip. It tasted light and sweet.

We walked back to the living room, sat in our seats and drank the tea in silence.

"What did you notice?" Veda asked, setting down her empty mug.

"I processed a series of questions," I said. "How long does water take to boil? How long does the tea take to steep? How long should I wait to drink the tea?"

"I noticed that the tea smelled like sweet apples," said Lucia. "The scent triggered a little gag for me."

"I felt impatient to taste the tea," said Simone. "And fidgety with all that silence."

"And the taste?" Veda asked.

"Oh yeah," Simone said. "Light and fruity."

Silence filled the air. Minutes passed as Veda looked out the window, breathing calmly.

Why isn't anyone talking? When is Veda going to continue? Is she trying to make us uncomfortable?

She looked at Simone, then Lucia.

Oh goodness, she's looking at me now. How long can humans stare into each other's eyes? My ears are burning. She's thinking about me, I know it. What is she thinking? I knew agreeing to this course was a bad idea.

"I'm curious," Veda said, breaking her eyes from mine. "What brings you each here?"

"I don't know what the next few months will hold for me," said Lucia. "But these women are my closest friends, and I need their support, so I can be present for the battle I'm fighting."

"I want to support my Lucy Lou," Simone said. "I also want to figure out what I should do about my job situation. I loved working with disadvantaged youth, so I'm feeling lost."

"As I've said before, this is all for Lucia," I said, rubbing my necklace charm.

Simone gave me an unconvinced look.

"What about feeling lost, empty and joyless?" Simone said. "That whole urge-to-escape thing?"

I crossed my arms and stared at Simone.

"Thank you for sharing, ladies," Veda said. "Let us practice what you came here to do: sit. You can choose from the mats, cushions, benches and blankets I have in the corner."

I chose a purple crescent cushion. Simone picked the gold padded wooden kneeling bench. Lucia chose the small yellow round cushion.

When I looked up from my cushion seat, I saw Veda on her knees, supported by a wooden T-shaped seat. It looked uncomfortable, but she seemed content with her eyes closed.

"Now we'll practice breathing and feeling our breath, first while we practice sitting, also known as meditation. After our sitting practice, we'll complete a body scan, moving our awareness from the bottoms of our feet to the top of our heads. At a couple points during our time, we'll gather to talk about our experiences. You'll also have time for a writing reflection near the end.

"As you sit, try to keep your knees below your hips. Place your hands on your thighs. Ensure you and your seat are stable. Keep your back upright but relaxed. Imagine sitting tall like a monarch. You have two options for your eyes: You can gaze downward a few feet in front of you, which I find keeps me grounded in the space. Or, you can close your eyes, which I find helps me focus more inwardly."

Veda guided us through the exercise. "Mindfulness is developed through meditation," she said. "In meditation, the objective isn't to avoid thinking. That will happen. We are tempted to ruminate about the past or run away, perhaps toward a distraction or 'planning mind,' and sometimes we become overwhelmed with feelings and become reactive to the emotion. Just come back to your breath each time you notice you've drifted off.

"Practice a slow, deep breath in now—feel the air enter your body, all those sensations in your nose, throat, chest and stomach. Now slowly release your breath through your mouth—noticing how the air feels passing over your lips and leaving your body. If you get distracted, just come back to your breath—noticing it as it naturally occurs.

"You can imagine your thoughts are bubbles. Touch them with a feather as they pass, but try not to pursue or grab them. They will pop! I sometimes practice slowing down the bubbles, watching them pass and naming what they are: 'Groceries,' 'Fight with my spouse,' 'Lesson plans,' and so forth. Just the act of naming them can make our thoughts less overwhelming and get us in touch with what's really occupying our mind. Some days, I may realize that most of my thoughts are about a certain aspect of my life—perhaps a particular relationship or work project. And I can look at that string of thoughts and think 'Isn't that interesting?'"

"What if I get caught up in thinking?" I asked.

"If you find yourself pursuing the thought bubbles, say in your mind, 'Thinking,' without judgment and come back to your breath," Veda said. "Another way I bring myself back if I find myself thinking is to tap one of my fingers on my leg or knee, wherever my hand is comfortably placed. It feels like my body is a bell and often makes me grin. Sometimes I will say a mantra, like 'Come home' or 'Just breathe.'

"Mindfulness is simply noticing what's inside and around you without judgment or attachment. Our breathing creates a bridge between what's inside—your mind, feelings, thoughts—and what's outside—your surroundings and other people. Our breath grounds us and helps us practice presence in a small, tangible, always-available way. In short, meditation is breathing deeply, ceasing to struggle, looking life in the face and relaxing as it is.

"Our mind's job is to think, plan and assess. We're not upset at the mind for doing its job, just remind our mind that she only needs to be present in the moment. I find it's helpful to tell my mind that she gets a vacation. I find it's also helpful to remember that my intent is to simply *be with what is*."

> **Posture Pointers**
>
> **Legs:** Knees below hips, legs loosely crossed (if applicable)
>
> **Hands:** Placed comfortably on thighs
>
> **Bottom:** Stable and centered
>
> **Spine:** Upright but relaxed
>
> **Chin:** Tucked slightly
>
> **Eyes:** Gaze downward gently, about five feet in front of you, which may help keep you in the moment. Or keep your eyes closed, which may help you focus inwardly.

"When we begin, I'll sound the meditation bowl once," Veda said. "When I sound it three times again, it signals the end of the sitting meditation."

Ding.

Thoughts flooded my mind.

OK, I'm meditating. Need to adjust on my seat. Breathe. What'd she say? I'm on vacation, my mind is on vacation. Vacation. Where should we go for spring break? When is Angelina's field trip? Did I get Bella signed up for choir? I don't know if I can hit the article deadline next week if the governor's communications director doesn't return my call. Vacation—mind on vacation. I'd kill for some lobster on vacation. Couldn't we just have lobster for dinner? What are we having for dinner? Ugh, I'm popping those thought bubbles. Thinking. I'll try tapping my leg. Breathe. Be with what is. What is going on with my legs? Are they going numb? My back certainly feels a little achy. I'm going to peek at my friends. Yep, they're all looking calm, eyes closed. Must just be me. How long are we going to sit here? Why are we just sitting quietly, again?

Ding, ding, ding.

We sat in silence for a full minute, then returned to the couch.

"What came up for you?" Veda asked.

"My legs were going numb, and my back was aching," said Simone.

"Mine, too," I replied. "And I felt impatient. Distracted, too. I kept thinking about my kids … and food."

"I kept thinking about my body and what it's fighting right now," said Lucia. "Fear kept coming up as I felt achiness coursing through my body."

We all nodded slowly as we looked at Lucia.

"Thank you for your vulnerability," Veda said, quietly. "We'll take a brief break, then begin the body scan."

I snuck my purse into the bathroom to check my messages. Pat texted, asking where the girls' swimming suits were.

How does this man not know where their swimming suits are?

Week 1: Sitting with Awareness

I responded and shoved the phone back in my purse before I walked out the door.

"Hey!"

I jumped. Simone stood in the hallway giving me a convicting look. Her eyes bounced to my purple purse.

"Checking messages, are we?"

"Just one," I said. "Pat couldn't find the girls' swimsuits."

"Sounds about right," Simone said. "Don't worry, I won't tell Veda … this time. Just get your head in the game, Meg."

After our break, we sat on our yoga mats, facing Veda.

Lucia has some pretty serious dark circles under her eyes. The cancer is taking its toll. I wonder how Simone and I can help her outside this breathing bootcamp?

"I invite you to lie down on your mat in Shavasana or corpse pose for our body scan practice." Veda said. "Lie on your back with your arms comfortably at your sides. Notice the sensations of your body and let go of any stories your mind tells.

"As before, I'll sound the meditation bowl once to signal the beginning of our next mindful practice," Veda said. "When I sound it three times again, it indicates the end of the body scan."

Ding.

"Bring your attention to your left foot," Veda said. "Feel your big toe, your second toe, middle, fourth and smallest toe.

"Notice your left ankle, left calf, knee, thigh, hip," she said.

Slowly moving from one body part to the next, I felt an ache in my left ankle.

That is from an old sprain playing basketball in high school. Wait, that's a story. My back feels relaxed, but my shoulders feel tight and my neck very stiff. I feel the air on my cheeks.

We ended at the tops of our heads.

Ding, ding, ding.

"We'll conclude with some writing, then a brief discussion. I bought you each journals, in your favorite colors: a purple one for Meghan, a sparkly one for Simone and a yellow journal for Lucia. You may use the space to free write about your experience today, such as what thoughts and emotions came up and the body sensations you experienced. Or you may write whatever you need to write about."

I opened my purple journal.

Who am I? What will make me happy? How do I rid myself of this echoing emptiness? Staying present in any moment feels like falling behind on every front of life. I'm so heartbroken about sweet Lucia that I can't sit with those thoughts for a moment or writing time will become weeping time. Why am I crying so much lately? Maybe I just need a vacation. An adventure. Something to relight the fire.

"Let's gather for a final discussion," said Veda. "What came up for you today physically, mentally, emotionally? Can you tell me about what you felt during the body scan?"

"I didn't realize I could feel air on my skin," I said. "And I've really missed writing for the pure joy of it."

"Yeah, I didn't realize I could make out the sensations of my scalp," Simone said.

"How about the writing exercise?" Veda asked.

"I guess it's a bit like meditation—writing connects me to what's going on inside and how I'm reacting to it," I said. "I've written my whole life and never thought about it as a meditation. But today I noticed I felt relaxed, focused and in tune with myself as I wrote. I felt my shoulders relax from my earlobes."

"How long should we meditate?" Lucia asked, feverishly scribbling out several lines of her journal writing.

"For homework this week, I invite you to practice sitting and body scanning every day," Veda said. "I also encourage you to consider the homework on the handout I'm giving you."

I read over the sheet.

Week 1 Homework: Sitting with Awareness (~10 minutes/day)

- **Awareness (3 min. to choose/practice):** Pick a routine habit and bring awareness to this activity (such as brushing teeth, lathering hair, washing dishes, smelling food or drink).
- **Sit (2 min.):** Practice sitting for 2 minutes daily.
- **Scan (2 min.):** Scan your body once per day (perhaps first thing in the morning or last thing before bed).
- **GLOWY Daily Reflection Practice (3 min.):** Write one page every morning (preferably outdoors) addressing the following:
    - **Gratitude:** Recognize things in your life that you're grateful for.

- **Lift Up:** Identify circumstances, people or struggles that are causing you/others to suffer; or needed wisdom/resources.
- **Observe:** Scan your body and notice sensations in your body, thoughts and feelings you're experiencing; observe your surroundings.
- **Wholesome Intention:** Set a clear, positive statement of the outcome you want to experience; how you intend to be, live and show up.
- **You Are:** Write positive affirmations about who you are.

- **Self-care:** Drink plenty of water daily to hydrate yourself, eat healthy and whole foods and get sufficient sleep each night.

One Time

- **Veda Hug:** Give someone you love a mindful hug. Don't let go until they do. Think about how grateful you are for them while they're in your arms.

Sweet mother of woo-woo, this looks like a lot of work.

"Do you have any tips for us?" Lucia asked.

"Set an intention for your practice and commit to daily practice," Veda said. "Self-care is a priority, so listen to your body and mind and nurture yourself."

"Does self-care include buying a new pair of shoes?" Simone asked.

"Sometimes, Simone," Veda said.

"I leave you with a blessing," Veda said, handing us each a stick of palo santo.

May you be happy.
May you be healthy.
May you be whole.
May you be peaceful.

With a slow bow, she left the room.

Sunday Lunch

All through service I kept thinking about Lucia. During the benediction, I leaned over and asked Pat if we could invite her over for lunch. He nodded. I shot her a text.

Me: Hey Lucia, I know it's last minute, but could you come over for lunch?

Lucia: What time?

Me: In an hour or so.

Lucia: I need a nap.

Me: You can sleep in our spare bedroom after lunch.

Lucia: Sounds great. Want me to bring anything?

Me: Just yourself.

Lucia's mom dropped her off at our house.

"I was too tired to drive," she said, as I opened the door.

We waved to her mom.

"What smells so good?" she asked.

"Pat's famous pot roast," I said. "Or as Simone calls it, posh roast."

"You've got to give me that recipe," she said. "Hi, Pat."

"Hey, Lucia," he said, handing her a glass of water. "I'm glad you could come over today."

"Hi, girls," she said. "Adriana has been begging for a play date. I'll chat with your mom and find a time."

"Yay!" the twins said in unison, running to the next room.

Lucia and I sat at the table while Pat finished lunch preparations.

"How are you?" I asked. "I'm worried about you and wanted to see what I can do to help."

"I appreciate it, Meg," she said. "I don't know what to tell you."

"Can I go to chemo with you?" I asked. "Is that allowed?"

"Sure, that would be great," she said. "How about Thursday morning?"

I checked my calendar.

"I'm wide open that morning, so count me in," I said. "Does it hurt, the chemo?"

"Not really. But it's pretty boring, so I get plenty of mindful practice in."

I stiffened.

"It's uncomfortable for you, isn't it?" she said. "The classes, I mean."

"I just can't shake the feeling that it's a foreign concept that doesn't jive with my beliefs."

"How so?" she asked.

"Like mindfulness requires that I believe in a different divine power and let go of how I interface with myself and God," I said. "That mindfulness takes the focus off serving God and turns the focus inward. It feels unindustrious, even a bit self-serving."

"I felt the same way when I was younger. I kept thinking that there was such a difference between the faith traditions of my family and what Veda, my godmother, taught me."

She took a sip of water.

"But you know what I discovered?" she asked.

I shook my head.

"They're really quite alike, just packaged a bit differently," she said. "And learning mindfulness makes me a better person, regardless of anything else."

"Hmmm," I said, furrowing my brow.

"Lunch is ready!" Pat called.

"I think you're brave," Lucia said to me.

"Me brave?" I said. "You're the one fighting cancer."

"All of life is being unsure," Lucia said. "But it takes courage to admit that uncertainty. And sit with it."

I felt a chill ascend my spine.

Chapter 4
Week 2: Awakening the Senses

Just watch this moment, without trying to change it at all. What is happening? What do you feel? What do you see? What do you hear?

—Jon Kabat-Zinn

The following Saturday, I awoke with a start. I'd forgotten to set my alarm. Rushing through my shower, I ran to the kitchen and grabbed a breakfast bar and poured yesterday's leftover coffee into a travel mug. I ran out the door, then realized I'd forgotten my phone. Searching in every conceivable spot, I finally found it in Angelina's room. I tiptoed out of her room and made it out the back door before anyone else awoke.

As I approached Veda's front door, I noticed it was cracked open. She had a sign on the door "Quiet please. Meditation in progress." Well, mine would be soon, even though I was fifteen minutes late. I entered the door quietly and saw that Veda and the other two were lying on their mats, already well into the body scan.

To mitigate the rustling, I just lay on the floor, forgoing my mat. Her carpet was surprisingly cushy, for which I was grateful.

I hope Angelina didn't wake up right after I left the house. Pat would be miffed about that. I wonder if they'll find the leftover banana bread for breakfast.

"Now breathe into your ribs," Veda said. "Feel your rib cage expand as your breath enters."

Ribs, yes. Oh no! I forgot to marinate the ribs for tonight's neighborhood cookout. Maybe I could sneak a quick text to Pat when we have a bathroom break.

"Bring your attention to your shoulders," Veda said. "Breathe into your shoulders."

Ack, did I completely miss the rest of my torso? Breathing into my shoulders. Wow, they are tight!

We finished the body scan with breathing into the top of our heads. Veda invited us to circle up.

"What came up for you during the body scan?" Veda asked. "Did any visitors, or thoughts, show up?"

"I kept thinking about how I needed a little pillow under my head," Simone said.

"What emotion are you feeling about that?" Veda asked. "And where do you feel it in your body?"

"I am frustrated that I didn't think about that before I lay down," Simone replied. "I feel the irritation in my neck."

"How about you, Meghan?" Veda asked.

"I struggled to focus," I said. "I was thinking about my family and how I forgot to marinate the ribs for dinner."

"What emotion are you feeling and how does your body feel?" Veda asked.

"I feel anxious," I replied. "I feel the stress in my tight shoulders and shallow breath."

"I was feeling pretty good until we got to the torso," Lucia said. "I felt scared, uncomfortable I guess, being with that area of my body."

"It can be difficult to let go of what's going on inside us and outside us," Veda said. "Challenging to bear witness to things as they are, such as an illness, a needed pillow, forgotten marinade."

Coming to Our Senses

"Today I'm going to let you in on a secret," Veda said. "You don't have five senses."

"Excuse me?" Simone said, as she raised her eyebrows and tilted her head forward.

"How many do you think you have?" Veda asked.

"I've always been taught I have five senses," I said. "Seeing, hearing, smelling, touching and tasting."

"Those are all correct," Veda said. "The secret is that you actually have six senses!"

"How's that?" Simone said, tilting her head to the left with a nod.

"You have the sense of your mind," she replied.

I should've seen that coming.

"Your mind senses an incredible number of stimuli," Veda said. "How you're feeling, what thoughts are running through your head."

"I'd never thought about the mind being one of our senses," said Lucia. "But it's logical, so I'm shocked we've never learned about that before."

"We'll have plenty of time today to explore with all *six* of our senses," Veda said. "Please join me in the kitchen."

On the beige countertop, I saw several ingredients—carrots, potatoes, garlic, broth, a unique dark brown sauce and some canned goods.

"Before we begin, let's take a few mindful breaths while we stand here," Veda said. "You might find it's more comfortable if you keep your legs shoulder-width apart, knees slightly bent, shoulders back, eyes looking forward."

I'm breathing in. I'm breathing out. I can't believe I forgot the marinade. I need to call Pat. He's going to be ticked. Thinking. Breathing in, my stomach expands and feels full when I take in air. Breathing out, the air tickles as it exits my lips.

"Now, let's begin," Veda said. "The mind is like these nutritious vegetables you see here, full of so much potential."

"But to bring about the full potential of the vegetables, we must marinate them in broth, so they may soften as they are cooked," Veda said. "Our mindful breath is like the broth, softening our mind, so it is supple to experience our life."

"Sounds delicious," said Simone. "Yes, ma'am, I have well-cooked brains."

We all laughed.

"I invite you to join me in making our lunch soup with these ingredients and this recipe," Veda said. "But I would like us to stay silent and follow this recipe. While you chop, stir and season, please breathe deeply and use your six senses.

"See the food you're touching, feel its texture, hear the sound it makes while you cut it and drop it into the broth. You may even sneak a taste."

"How do we know who's doing what in the recipe?" I asked. "I love garlic, but we probably don't want twelve cloves in the soup."

"Thank you for asking," Veda said. "Please put your initials next to the steps you'll be tackling. Oh, and remember to remain aware of your friends. Even though you'll be silent, you can see them, smell them as they walk by you. Keep all your senses alive.

"Select your first ingredient. I recommend it's something you want to touch and taste. I'll guide you through a sensory exploration."

Sensory Exploration

Sight: Look at the ingredient. What do you see?

Touch: Pick it up and notice how it feels.

Hear: How does the ingredient sound?

Smell: Now smell it. How would you describe the scent?

Taste: You may taste it. How would you describe the flavor?

Mind: Lastly, what are you thinking as you experience this ingredient?

I picked up the first carrot, cold from the fridge. I sniffed it and began peeling it, listening to the sound of the *shhhh-k*. Breaking off a chunk of carrot, I tasted it.

Bright and very crunchy. As a carrot top myself, I appreciate this colorful vegetable.

"Please complete the recipe in silence and keep your senses alert. I'll chime in regularly to remind you of a sense to pull into focus."

We worked silently.

I hear the sssshhhh-chk *of my knife cutting the onion. It is a strong onion. I feel my eyes sting and am fighting the urge to wipe away the tears.*

"Experience the ingredients like an explorer in a new land," Veda said. "What would you write back to your colleagues and loved ones about these ingredients?"

After some silence, she continued.

"Before you pick up an ingredient, remember to look at it," Veda said. "Then feel it when you pick it up, its texture, shape and girth."

"Let us pause for a moment to experience the broth," Veda said. "Remember that the broth represents the breath that will soften our thoughts, or ingredients."

She passed the carton for us to see its container, feel its weight and smell the broth.

"Watch and listen," Veda said, pouring the caramel-colored liquid into the slow cooker with a quiet splatter.

Veda bent over to smell it. She dipped a spoonful of the broth, swishing it in her mouth like a fine wine. She handed us each a soup spoon, and we followed suit.

It's salty yet blander than I expected.

One by one we began adding our ingredients to the slow cooker. *Plop, plop.*

Veda stirred the ingredients together and turned it on high. She invited us to look at what we'd created.

"Thank you for your help," Veda said. "We will enjoy our soup later on. For now, let's practice sitting."

Sitting in Silence

I sat on my knees with a purple crescent cushion between my legs. Simone sat cross-legged like Veda, while Lucia sat on a padded chair.

"Settle into your seat," Veda said. "Remember that the mind's job is to think. You don't need to judge it for doing its job. When you notice your mind wandering, gently bring your attention back to your breath. As I've mentioned before, you might consider tapping your leg twice and using a mantra like 'Just breathe' or 'Come home' or 'Practicing.' Whatever best serves you."

Ding.

Already this sitting session is going better. I feel steady on the buckwheat-filled cushion on top of my Mexican blanket. This is going to be a great sit. Oh, I'm thinking. I'll tap my leg twice. Practicing. Can't believe I forgot the marinade.

I heard a *ding*, but it wasn't Veda's musical bowl. It was my cell phone. I looked over at my purse.

Ack! I forgot to turn off my phone. I bet it's Pat texting. Oh, my phone just dinged again. Should I breathe or turn off my phone?

After what seemed like forever I heard Veda's musical bowl.

Ding, ding, ding.

Shew.

"Let's gather in the next room to talk for a few minutes," Veda said.

I ran to my purse, opened it, carefully pushing around a thick stack of papers I didn't want anyone to see. I turned off the sound. It was Pat, asking about dinner.

I sent Pat a quick text: "Please marinate ribs."

After we sat down, I shifted from side to side, avoiding eye contact with my friends.

"What came up for you during our sitting practice?" Veda asked.

"Besides Meghan's phone dinging?" Simone asked with a half-serious smirk as she looked at me. "Didn't you learn anything from the Queen Alba story?"

"I'm so sorry," I said. "When I heard my phone, I felt my shoulders tense up and my arms draw in. I held my breath, dreading the next ding."

"Sometimes visitors come in a variety of costumes," Veda replied.

"You keep mentioning visitors," Lucia said. "What do you mean by that?"

"A visitor can be an actual person, or a thought, emotion or physical sensation," Veda explained.

"I like that word, visitor," Lucia said. "It's interesting how that word can have a good or bad connotation."

"We can practice just being with visitors of all types," Veda said. "Not labeling visitors as good or bad."

She stood up.

"Let's go outside for an exercise. Please bring your journals."

Week 2: Awakening the Senses

As we stepped outdoors, I caught a glimpse of an enormous tree with a staircase zigzagging up one side of it and perched atop of it was a treehouse. Not just any treehouse—a treehouse with a door, windows, siding and even a mailbox.

"Are you expecting a visitor?" Simone asked Veda, with a wink.

"Well, yes," she replied, chuckling. "Sometimes my granddaughter Ruth visits, and we play for hours up there."

"How sweet," Lucia said. "That's a fun hideout."

"You've already begun our practice of seeing," Veda said. "Please join me in sitting on this bench for five minutes. Your only focus is to see what's around you."

"Do you want us to write what we see?" Lucia asked.

"Not for now," Veda said. "Just sit and open your eyes to see all that's here."

Ding.

I notice a large pine tree, probably ten feet tall.

I see an acre of barren cornfield, filled with mounds of moist churned dirt.

I notice a light-brown stone the size of a baseball but shaped like an egg.

I look down next to my foot and see something that's fallen from a tree; it looks like a prickly golf ball, an orb packed with baby bird beaks, open with hunger. I hear them say, "Tweet, tweet, please feed me, Mama."

The basketball goal looks weathered, its red lines faded to a light pink. I imagine family and friends have had many memories here. The net is still intact and swishes to the left with the breeze. Mother nature shoots ... and scores!

"Now, choose one thing you'd like to see more closely," Veda said. "Once you've chosen it, walk to it and inspect it."

I chose the pine tree.

I walked across the driveway, past the basketball goal and reached the tree. It was taller than I estimated, probably twelve or fourteen feet tall. I looked at its base, then slowly all the way to its top. The top swayed very slightly in the wind. The tree was wide and full of deep green, spiky foliage. I moved my head closer. Oww! It pricked my nose like a handful of needles. My eyes watered, and I struggled to see clearly for a few moments. When my vision returned, I saw tiny caramel-colored buds. How cute!

Ding, ding, ding.

"Please join me on the bench," Veda said.

We sat down on the bench, looking up at Veda for our next instruction.

"You are free to write your visual observations for the next five minutes," she said.

I noticed Lucia staring at me. I smiled awkwardly in return.

Ding.

I began writing: *I know this was just a seeing exercise, but I felt something deep for that pine tree. It held the freshness of fallen snow. The majesty of a Norwegian prince. The smell of eternal winter. Its needles, hunter green, ridged and shiny, enjoy an elegant point at their end. They look like dainty eagle talons. I recently learned the word twiglet, another name for sprig. Sounds like piglet and makes me giggle. The twiglet feels like springy fur, maybe like a hedgehog, when you pet it with the grain. Relaxing even. But don't be fooled. They'll still stab you and make you cry if you approach them*

Week 2: Awakening the Senses

with brutish or naïve enthusiasm. Its buds, tender and easy to miss, form miniature blooming pyramids that hold the mystery of nature and the promise of new life.

Ding, ding, ding.

I took a deep breath and swore I smelled the pine tree. Perhaps the smell was trapped in my nostrils. That thought made me smile.

"Please join me inside," Veda said.

I took one last look at the pine tree, then decided to run back to it. Surely, I could find a small sprig of it for my nature collection, a reminder of our time together. I circled the tree and right before I gave up hope, I saw a three-inch sprig on the ground. I snatched it and brought it to my nose for a deep smell.

Ahh, so lovely. Oww! You'd think I'd learned my lesson!

I stepped into the basement and headed up the stairs. Half-way up the stairs I was greeted with a face full of smell. Oh, the soup! It smelled marvelous. When I rounded the corner at the top of the stairs, I saw all the women gathered around the slow cooker smelling it. Veda was stirring.

"The soup needs a bit more time to cook," Veda said. "Let's enjoy a longer sitting practice while we wait."

After we all took a long whiff, we headed to the basement for the sitting practice.

Sitting. I wonder how long a "longer" sitting practice is. Knowing Veda, probably forty-five minutes. I can't sit still for forty-five minutes. No, Meg, you've got this. One deep breath at a time. I can smell the soup. I feel my stomach growling. The beautiful pine tree, so tall. I'm slouching. I need to sit up tall. That's better.

"Sometimes our minds wander when our bodies are still," Veda. "When you notice this happening, simply come back home to your breath."

Yep, my mind is wandering. I need to come home to my breath. Whatever that means. Probably just breathe.

I adjusted my position on the cushion, sneaking a look at Lucia. She was grabbing her left shoulder with a wince.

This is for Lucia, however physically and mentally overwhelming it is. My nose stings a bit from the pine tree. I wonder if I could convince Pat to plant a pine tree in our yard. Probably not. He's too busy. Too busy to make breakfast. Too busy to kiss me goodbye. Too busy to come home for dinner. But, he is helping with the twins, so I can be here. I wonder if he'll be on his phone all day. I'm not there. I'm here.

Ding, ding, ding.

"I can't wait to eat the soup," Lucia said.

"How about we don't wait any longer," Veda said. "Let's chat while we eat."

"I love the way you think," Simone said.

Veda slowly dished up our soup as we walked through the line one by one.

"Please wait to eat until we've all sat down," Veda said.

After the three of us sat at the table, Veda joined us.

WEEK 2: AWAKENING THE SENSES

"I'm grateful for getting to spend time with each of you," Veda said. With her hands in a traditional prayer position, she bowed her hands toward us with a nod, one at a time.

Veda invited us to take our first five spoonfuls in silence, slowly and with our senses wide open.

My mouth watered as I lifted the first spoonful to my mouth. I smelled the carrots and potatoes. When I took my first bite, I realized it was still a little hot for me. I waited a few moments. My eyes wandered to Simone's face. She gave me a "What are you looking at?" look. I smiled wide and took my next bite. This time I tasted more garlic and onion.

"Now, tell me about your day," Veda said. "What came up for you?"

"I enjoyed cooking together," Simone said. "It was a unique experience cooking with other people in silence."

"The seeing and writing exercise was my favorite thus far," I said. "I never noticed how adorable pine tree buds are."

I showed them my sprig.

"And I noticed how distracting it was to keep thinking about forgetting to marinate the ribs."

"Mercy," Simone said. "You are so flustered that *I* feel worried about those blasted ribs."

We all laughed.

"It felt holy to prepare our meal in silence," Lucia said. "It reminded me of communion at my church."

"Speaking of communion, has your mom come home from church this week?" Simone said.

"Barely," Lucia said, shaking her head. "Ever since Mama learned about my cancer diagnosis, she has camped out at our church. I'm not sure there are enough prayer candles in the world for her."

"I didn't realize you'd told your parents already," Veda said. "I would've gone with you."

Lucia nodded and her eyes glistened.

"I just sensed the timing was right this last week," Lucia said. "When Mama returned from Wednesday evening's service, it felt like she already knew."

"That gives me goosebumps," Simone said. "I think your Mama has a *seventh* sense: knowing everything."

"You may be right about that one, Simone." Lucia said.

"I'm proud of you for having the courage to show up and be vulnerable like that with your family," I said.

"It makes me think of the word 'visitor' again," Lucia said. "I understand that cancer is a visitor in my body right now. I also see that my mother is a visitor in her church … perhaps a permanent visitor. I just hope this cancer isn't a permanent visitor."

"We hope not, too, Lucia," I said, putting my hand on Lucia's forearm.

I scanned our homework sheet. It looked similar to last week, except for a looking exercise: Look at your face in the mirror. Notice one thing and write about it in your journal.

I bet I'll notice several things like fine lines, wrinkles and freckles.

"Next week we will practice mindful movement," Veda said.

Week 2: Awakening the Senses

Veda concluded with a blessing. "Today's blessing is from Zen Master Thich Nhat Hanh."

May you be fresh as a flower.
May you be strong as a mountain.
May you be calm as the water.
May you be free as the sky.

Lucia's phone buzzed.

"I guess I forgot to turn off my phone, too," Lucia said. She grabbed her phone. "It's Mama. She's worried about me."

"May I hug you?" Veda asked Lucia.

"I'm always open for a Veda hug," Lucia responded. "They are truly magical."

The automatic glass doors opened, allowing Lucia and me to enter the large hospital lobby. High ceilings and mauve walls served as a backdrop to beige artforms that swooped above our heads and down the hallway to the elevators.

I'm fine, Lucia's fine. Chemo will help lengthen her life. I wonder if she's scared. Be strong, Meg. Lucia needs you.

As we exited the elevator onto the third floor, Lucia stumbled a bit. I grabbed her before she fell to the ground.

"My neuropathy is worsening," she said. "It's hard to feel my feet when I walk."

A young nurse greeted us.

"Welcome, Lucia," she said. "Who is your friend?"

"This is Meghan."

"I'm glad you could join Lucia today," she said. "Please follow me."

She led us past a fireplace to Lucia's treatment area. A beige leather reclining chair was flanked by a guest chair. A pull curtain was pushed back, available to separate her from the patients on either side, if she wanted.

"Please make yourselves comfortable," she said.

So this is where it happens, in a leather chair overlooking a succulent garden on a terrace. Four feet from an older gentleman on one side and teenage girl on the other. At least there's a TV.

Once we got settled, the nurse came back to start the process.

"I'm going to numb the skin above your port with a needle, just like last time," she said cheerily.

Lucia pulled back her shirt collar a bit. Once numb, the nurse connected a tube to a port in her skin, just below her collarbone. I followed the tube to the hanging bag of fiery red liquid.

Red means danger. What exactly is this medicine? What is that fluid doing to Lucia?

Lucia caught my eye.

"This is Adriamycin," she said.

"Looks scary," I said.

Meg, you are supposed to be strong and positive. Hold it together.

Week 2: Awakening the Senses

"They call it the red devil," she said, "because it's bright red."

"How long will it take?"

"Probably about three hours today."

Three hours? How am I going to stay focused and not freaked out for that long? Small talk. And there's always the TV.

"I've been doing a little research on mindfulness," I said. "I learned that it can help regulate emotions and help decrease stress, anxiety and even depression."

"Do you feel it's done that for you?"

"I don't know," I said. "I'm still pretty stressed with all that's on my plate."

The incessant beeping began to give me a headache.

"Do you still want to run away?" she asked.

"What?" I said. "No. Why do you ask?"

"You have that look in your eye."

"Sometimes it feels like being mindful, present with life, increases stress and anxiety," I said. "Like right now, it's all I can do not to break down crying every moment I stop to think about what you're going through. How a red devil is running through your veins doing God knows what. How a little mass of rogue cells is invading your body."

My eyes stung.

"Hi, Lucia!"

We looked to the right to see a man, probably in his seventies, waving from the next treatment station. Though his skin hung from his face, pale and gray, he smiled kindly.

"Hi, Frank."

"How's my chemo buddy today?" he asked.

"I'm alright," Lucia said. "My friend Meghan is joining me today."

"Nice to meet you, Meghan," he said. "Where are you from? You look familiar."

"The east side."

A loud bell rang merrily.

"What was that?" I asked.

"Tom just finished chemo," Frank said. "So he gets to ring the brass bell that hangs on the wall."

I wonder if Lucia will ever get to ring that bell? I'm scared to know the answer.

I shuddered.

Lucia gave me a concerned look. A hunched-over volunteer pushing a cart paused between us and Frank.

"Would you like to borrow a magazine, book or puzzle?"

She held up a Sudoku book with an inviting smile.

"No thanks," Lucia responded. Frank waved his pass.

I scanned her book collection.

I'd give anything to escape into a book right now.

"Anyway," said Frank. "I'm from the east side, too, born and raised. Did you go to East Central?"

"Yeah."

"Me too," he said. "You know, I dated a redhead in high school. She looked a lot like you."

I blushed.

"Her name was Cora, but I was really in love with her sister, Veda," Frank said. "Unfortunately she ran off to California after high school, and I never got a chance to win her heart."

Lucia and I locked eyes.

"That wouldn't happen to be Veda Hazeldine?" Lucia asked. "Or Lombardi was her maiden name, I think."

Frank sat up.

"You know her?"

"She's my godmother."

"I loved Veda to my core and never forgot her all these years," he said. "In fact …"

He reached into his pocket.

"I gave her a heart-shaped stone when we were young and kept a matching one for myself," he said. "I didn't have much money at the time, but I wanted her to know that my love for her would never change, like the stones."

He pulled out two rough half-dollar-sized brown stones.

"She gave hers back to me when she got engaged to some foo-foo artist or writer, something like that," he said. "I've carried these in my pocket every day."

He looked away, out onto the lush terrace.

"The stones remind me of her exceptionally magnificent aura and all that's good and right in this world."

He touched the port over his heart and was silent for several moments. He glanced at Lucia.

"Sometimes things don't turn out like we hope," he said.

"Adriana!" my twins yelled, running to her on the large, colorful playground. After some hugs, the three girls began swinging side by side.

The tall curly slide sat next to the shaky wooden bridge. Just past the wooden bridge sat a pyramid-shaped spinning climbing rope. A metal perch offered some drums to play, and the monkey bars snaked right and left, with a slight pitch upward.

"Thank you for setting up a play date," Lucia said, sitting on a bench in the shade, a few yards from the edge of the playground.

"Here's Simone and her kids," I said, waving and joining Lucia on the bench.

"Ladies," Simone greeted, pulling out a pint of *tres leches* ice cream and three spoons from her purse.

"You know the kids are going to swarm us, right?" I said.

Week 2: Awakening the Senses

"I told them if they pestered us, we would leave immediately," she said.

"Brilliant," I said.

"I have my moments."

"How did you find *tres leches* ice cream?" Lucia asked, getting a big scoop.

"I drove clear to the west side of town," she said. "Good thing I love you."

"Bella, please wait your turn," I yelled.

"Watch this," Simone said, running to the playground. She climbed up to the monkey bars and made it four rungs before dropping and walking back to us.

"Shew, that's harder than I remember," she said. "I think I burnt enough calories for a few more scoops."

We chuckled with ice cream melting in our mouths.

"Lucia, I need an update," Simone said. "Don't make me go all Detective Meg on you with a hundred questions. Just spill the beans."

"Meg joined me at chemo this week," she said.

"No fair, my turn next time," Simone said, digging her spoon into the ice cream. "Sorry, please continue."

"We learned Veda has a secret admirer," I said.

"Oh, I've gotta hear about this," Simone said. "Who's her admirer?"

"Frank," Lucia said. "A high school flame of sorts. Frank is a chemo buddy of mine."

"The mystery continues," Simone said. "As much as I want the scoop on this Frank, Lucia, I want to hear about you more."

"I'm tired and have about maxed out my PTO to go to chemo and rest," she said. "Excuse me for a second."

She ran to the line of bushes and vomited. She slowly walked back our way.

"And you're tossing *tres leches*," Simone said, handing her a napkin.

"Yeah," she said, wiping her mouth. "That makes for a fun day when I'm actually at work. Timing lunch and meetings with my puking schedule is a part-time job."

"Is there anything that helps?" I asked.

"Seeing you two," Lucia said. "And learning from Veda."

"Mmmmkay, so since we're on the topic of Veda," Simone said. "Who is this lady? I'm not entirely convinced she's from planet Earth. No one in their right mind is that calm all the time."

"Veda is Veda," Lucia said.

"My dad said the same thing when I asked him about her," I said.

"What's that mean—'Veda is Veda'?" Simone asked.

"She's let the tragedy of life make her strong in the right ways," Lucia said. "She's chosen love, kindness and stillness as a way of being."

"What tragedy?" I asked.

"I'm sorry, friends, I'm really tired," Lucia said. "Let's save that conversation for another day. Thank you for the ice cream, Simone. I'll see you two on Saturday."

When Lucia and Adriana drove off, Simone turned to me with a raised eyebrow.

"Something's up," Simone said. "Besides cancer and chemo."

"I feel the same way," I said. "Think we should corner her for questioning?"

"Gang up on a chemo patient," Simone said. "I thought you'd never ask."

Chapter 5
Week 3: Mindful Movement

Meditation is more about a balance between inside and outside, an ease in your body, an acceptance of whatever is taking place, and an ability to be quiet, listen and let go.

—Ginny Figlar and Gaiam Staff

This Saturday began much more smoothly than last week. My alarm went off at 5:30 a.m. After a hot shower and a breakfast sandwich, I left my husband a note.

Good morning, hon. Thank you for taking care of getting the kids to your parents' today. I know you have a full day. I appreciate all you do for us and the support you give me. You know, one thing I love about you is how your big brown eyes sparkle when the kids make you laugh. It's really sweet. I did marinate the kabobs for tonight's cookout. Simone and her kids will arrive around 6 and Lucia can come a little later. If you could pick up some tangerines, I'll give you 17 kisses. See you this evening. Love, Meg

I pulled up to Veda's house and saw Simone getting out of her pearl-white Cadillac SUV.

"Mornin', Simone," I said.

"Mornin', Meghan," she said with a wink.

I saw a note on the basement door for us to enter. As we stepped inside the basement, I saw Veda and Lucia sitting cross-legged on their yoga mats, facing one another as they spoke in hushed tones.

"Whenever you're ready, Lucia," Veda whispered.

Veda looked up and greeted us.

"Welcome, ladies," she said.

"*Buenos días, chicas*," I said. "Am I on time?"

"Yes, Lucia and I are just catching up a bit," Veda responded. "Please join us on your mats."

Simone laid out her gold sparkle mat.

"I didn't know they sold gold sparkly mats," I said.

"You know what they say," Simone said. "It ain't a thing unless it's got some bling."

Simone smiled and pumped her eyebrows up and down quickly.

"Today we'll be practicing mindful movement," Veda said. "We'll explore floor movement, standing movement and walking. If you are unable to do any of these exercises, you're invited to visualize the movements."

"Good thing I ate my Wheaties this morning," Simone said, stretching her arms to the sky with a yawn.

"I could use some coffee," I said.

"Me, too," Lucia said.

"Let's take a couple breaths to experience the feelings of wanting that we may be having," Veda said.

After a few moments, Veda asked, "How about some tea?"

"I guess that'll work," I said. "Got anything leaded?"

"I know just the thing!" Veda said.

Tea Time

In the kitchen, Veda sat the kettle on the stove. She scooped dried tea leaves into her turquoise ceramic steeping pot. She raised it to my nose. I took a long breath in. It smelled unlike any tea I'd ever tried. Simone and Lucia took a smell, also.

"What is that?" I asked.

"Oolong," Veda answered.

"It smells a little coconutty," I said.

"Indeed it does," Veda said. "Oolong is a tea that's neither black nor green. It's in a category all of its own. This particular tea is blended with coconut."

"Sassy and sweet," Simone said. "That's my kind of tea."

Veda poured the boiling water over the tea leaves. For a moment, we stood silently, staring at the tea pot as if willing it to steep by our attention.

After about three minutes, Veda poured our tea into turquoise cups without handles. I felt the heat blaze through the ceramic cups.

"Oh, hot!" I exclaimed, setting it back on the countertop.

Veda lifted her cup to her nose and took a long breath, then sat her cup on the countertop, as well.

"While it cools, let's stretch our arms to the sky, just like Simone did before we came upstairs for a spot of tea," Veda said, dinging her teacup with her spoon to begin our practice and then reaching her hands up to the sky. Lucia only stretched a little.

"With this and all movements we practice, listen to your body and only do what makes sense for you," Veda said. "If a movement or position feels uncomfortable, try breathing into the area that's experiencing discomfort. If it's still too much, back out of the position partially or completely. You can always practice breathing while sitting, standing or in corpse pose, or simply visualize the movements."

Wow, does this stretch feel amazing. My left shoulder feels tight.

"This stretch is always available to you," Veda said. "It's a good one to get blood flowing first thing in the morning, even before you get out of bed, if you like."

Lucia tilted her head to the right, then to the left.

"Lucia is leading us into the second movement," Veda said with a smile. "Please show us again."

She tilted her head to the right, then left, with everyone following her lead.

I stretched my right arm across my body and pressed it with my left hand, then repeated the move with my left arm.

"Our third movement is brought to you by Meghan," Veda said. "I'll let you demonstrate."

I repeated the shoulder stretch.

WEEK 3: MINDFUL MOVEMENT

All my laptop typing must be making my neck and shoulders tight. It probably has nothing to do with raising twins and running a household with a husband who works long hours.

When I looked up, Veda was bent over at the waist, exhaling and letting her arms fall toward the ground.

"This is ragdoll pose," Veda said in a constricted voice. She inhaled as she stood up, reaching her arms to the sky, then exhaled as she bent over again.

Simone and I mirrored her movements. Lucia stood with her eyes closed.

Veda stood up and pressed her arms back behind her, opening her chest to the ceiling.

What a glorious stretch; I feel the stretch up my neck to my lower jaw.

"Ahh, now who wants tea?" Veda asked.

After enjoying our oolong tea, delightful with its dessert-like coconut flavor, we returned to the basement.

"I invite you to lie on your back on your mat in Shavasana, or corpse pose," Veda said.

"Creepy," Simone whispered with wide eyes.

Lucia and I met eyes and shook our heads.

"Let your arms lie at your sides, palms up," Veda said. "Notice where your body is touching the floor. Perhaps the sensations on the back of your head, upper back, hands, buttocks, calves and heels."

I feel the most pressure on the back of my head and heels. I might need some extra cushion.

"If you feel discomfort, you may choose to be with that discomfort or address it," Veda said. "Perhaps with a blanket under your hips, head or other body part."

I placed a blanket under my hips and another under my head.

"Scan your body from head to toe, noting places where you may be holding tension," Veda said. "See if you can soften any of those places."

I noticed my shoulders were tensed up toward my ears. I let them relax a bit.

"Notice your breath," she said. "Feel your belly expanding and falling.

"Let us set an intention for today's practice. This may be: 'I intend to move with mindfulness, paying attention to my body and noticing what comes up in my mind and heart.'"

Intentions are like to-do lists. I set my intention to stay present in my body as I move and to fully feel my body's movements.

Ding.

"We'll begin with what I call rock-a-bye," Veda said. "Bend your left knee to the sky, then your right knee to the sky. Hold your knees with your hands. Inhale and relax your knees away from your body. Exhale and pull your knees closer to your chest. Notice where you feel the sensations, perhaps in your back and buttocks, or through the backs of your shoulders as you stretch your arms around your knees.

"Remember that if a position doesn't honor your body, you can always practice breathing while sitting or in corpse pose," Veda said.

I practiced allowing my breath to guide my movement: exhale and bring knees in, inhale and move knees out.

Week 3: Mindful Movement

It is a bit more challenging to reach around my knees than I expected. But the rocking movement feels like a nice back massage.

"Now release your hands," Veda said.

I heard a *clump* as Lucia's feet hit the floor.

"And slowly let your feet release to the floor, left foot first, then right. Keep your legs bent and your feet near your buttocks.

"With your knees bent, using your hips, tilt to touch the small of your back to your mat three times. You may notice your stomach muscles engaging to complete this movement. Release and come back to neutral. Repeat. Now as you keep your upper torso grounded, push your weight into your heels and lift your hips off the ground for a bridge. We'll do this three times."

I couldn't remember the last time I'd done a bridge. I felt my glutes engage, and I wobbled a bit on my upper torso.

"For our last movement on our backs today, please place your right ankle on top of your left thigh. Pull your left thigh toward your chest with both hands. If it feels right for your body, use your right elbow to press your bent right leg back a bit. Release your left leg to the ground and switch legs, left ankle on top of right thigh. Pull your right thigh toward your chest."

Wow, my hamstrings are tight. I really need to stretch after I run.

"Gradually turn over onto your stomach. Then get on your hands and knees, with your knees under your hips and your hands on the mat below your shoulders," Veda instructed. "We call this tabletop.

"Notice the sensations of your hands and knees on the mat. You can place a blanket under your knees for padding, if needed.

"Now exhale as you move your head towards the floor and your middle back toward the sky, making the letter C with your body," she said. "Then inhale as you arch your back, letting your spine curve toward the floor and your head move toward the sky. This is called cat-cow."

After a few cat-cows, Veda led us into child's pose.

"Move your hips on top of your ankles and let your upper body move toward the floor. Lengthen your arms out straight above your head, away from your body. If possible, bring your forehead to the floor. Notice the sensations and remember to listen to your body. If ever any position is too much, please back out of it.

"Return to tabletop, knees under hips and hands under shoulders.

"Now, gradually move into a sitting position, legs crossed. Place your left hand on the ground and reach your right arm over your head and lean to your left. You may feel a pulling up your right side. As you stretch, clench your right hand tightly, then release it. Repeat this three times. Now, roll your right wrist in one direction. Now the other direction. Release your right hand to the ground. Now reach your left arm over your head and lean to the right. Clench your left hand tightly, then release it. Repeat this three times. Roll your left wrist in one direction. Now in the other direction.

"Place the bottoms of your feet together. Let your knees fall open. This is cobbler's pose. Sit up tall. You might use your thumbs to massage the bottoms your feet. You can try opening your feet like a book for an added stretch."

It had never occurred to me to open my feet like a book and massage them. The massage felt nice. And a bit poetic that the soles of our feet can open like a book, a unique story.

Week 3: Mindful Movement

"Softly place your palms on your thighs—right hand on your right thigh, left hand on your left thigh. Sit up tall, with your eyes closed if that serves you, and breathe deeply for three breath cycles. Notice how you have met your intention of mindful movement."

Ding, ding, ding.

"Let's take a brief break," Veda said. "We'll then practice mindful movement while standing, as well as a walking meditation."

From my mat, I greeted Lucia.

"*Hola*," I said.

"Hey, Meghan."

"How are you feeling this week?" I asked, as Simone joined us on my mat.

"OK," Lucia replied. "All this movement today is wearing me out. I'm awaiting next steps from my doctor, and Mama is freaked out."

"Is she still going to church every day?" I asked.

"Absolutely," Lucia said. "And my niece Adriana is starting to ask why my mama is so sad all the time. And why I take more naps. I don't know what to tell her. Adriana's only eight. I want to be honest with her ... about everything. But I'm not sure about the balance between what she should know and what's too much."

"That's tough," Simone said. "Since Anthony and I split when Xavier was young, I understand that struggle of balancing truth with the limits of their maturity."

"What about you, Simone, how's the job search coming along?" Lucia asked.

"Still looking," Simone said. "With two kids and no husband in the household, it's a stressful situation. Luckily Anthony is a great dad and our parents help how they can. I have so many ideas I'd like to implement to help kids in need. I saw myself working that job for the rest of my life. Practicing mindfulness has helped me see that my heart is still with disadvantaged youth.

"Enough about me," Simone said. "Meghan, how you doin'? Any great escapes planned?"

"No, I just landed a big account, which was a key determining factor in my decision to launch a communications business, like I mentioned a few weeks ago," I said. "I'm thinking about business names, so I can get registered with the state. Open to ideas, ladies."

Why can't I tell them what's really going on? Lucia has too much on her plate. I can't burden her with any more.

"Let me think on that," Simone said. "But, hey, I've been thinking we should invite Veda and her mythical husband to Meghan's cookout tonight. Do you think he's hiding in their bedroom? Probably doing a sitting meditation the whole time we're here."

Simone closed her eyes and touched her thumbs to her index fingers.

Lucia and I shook our heads as we smiled at Simone's speculations.

Moving Mindfully

Veda returned and invited us to stand.

"We'll begin in mountain pose," she said. "Standing with our feet shoulder-width apart, knees slightly bent, pelvis slightly tilted under."

Ding.

WEEK 3: MINDFUL MOVEMENT

"Feel your feet, all four corners of your feet," she said, slowly shifting her weight around the edges of her feet in a circle fashion. "Ground yourself through your planted feet and deepening breath.

"Lean your head to the left, then gradually roll it back, then to the right, then to the front. Now reverse, to the right, back, left and front.

"Come back to center. Let's pause for a breath in mountain pose. With your palms facing in, raise your arms straight in front of your body, parallel to the ground, breathing in. Release your arms slowly to your sides while you breathe out. Let's repeat this a few times, letting our in-breath guide our hands up, and our out-breath guide our hands back to our sides."

Now this is calming.

"Now let's raise our arms out to our sides, to form a T," Veda said. "Turn your palms up to face the sky. Breathe out as you curl your arms in and touch your shoulders. I call this move two worlds. Breathing in, extend into a T, breathing out, touching your shoulders.

"I invite us back to mountain pose. We will move like we are lowering ourselves into a seat for chair pose," Veda said. "Bend at the knees, and gradually, with your palms facing inward, raise your hands up to the sky as you move your buttocks back into the imaginary chair. Slowly return to mountain pose and repeat chair pose, noticing where you are feeling the stretch. Return to mountain pose.

"From mountain pose, shift your weight to your left leg, and raise your right thigh parallel to the ground, knee bent. Now extend that right leg and point your toes out in front of you. Breathing out, bring your leg back in, bending it at the knee. Breathing in, extend that leg again, pointing your foot. Breathing out, return it to the raised, bent-knee position. Return your right leg to the ground. Now let's do that on the other side."

I almost lost my balance on that one.

I saw Lucia standing still in mountain pose, eyes closed.

She's taking a pass on this move. I'm glad she's not pushing herself too hard.

"Lift your left thigh parallel to the floor, bending at the knee. Extend your left leg and point your toes as you breathe out. Bring your left leg back in, bending it at the knee and breathing in. Extend it again, breathing out. Now plant it back on the ground, and let's return to mountain pose.

"Placing our hands on our hips, we will draw a large circle around our body with our head by leaning our torso forward at the waist then moving it around. Imagine a marker on the top of your head drawing a circle in the air as you breathe in and slowly lean to your left, then lean back, keeping that circle smooth, then to your right, and back to the front. Now we'll return in the opposite direction, breathing out."

That was one wiggly circle. I'll need to practice that movement.

"With your arms at your side reach your hands toward the floor as you stand up tall. Spread your fingers out wide. Slowly bring your arms up to a T, then above your head, reaching toward the sky. Hold it here for a couple breaths. Touch your palms together in prayer hands and bring your hands down in front of your heart.

"Namaste," Veda said, bowing deeply.

"Namaste," we replied, bowing.

That word still feels weird to me.

Ding, ding, ding.

"I invite you to take a few deep breaths before we begin our walking meditation," Veda said.

"In walking meditation, we are focusing on our body as we walk, all the sensations, movements, shifting of weight, even aches and pains that we may overlook in our daily lives. The purpose is to be fully present with our walking, knowing that we are walking, just for the sake of walking, without hurrying. Walking in peace, we are kissing the earth with our feet.

"Starting in mountain pose, legs shoulder-width apart. Feel all four corners of your feet by gently shifting your weight around," she said, shifting her weight around the edges of her feet in a circular fashion. "Feel the ground below your feet supporting you.

"Slowly take a step with your right foot. Experience the sensation of the planted foot rolling forward as you shift your weight forward. Feel the various elements of your step. Notice how your hips shift to support your intention to walk, how your arms swing and perhaps touch your sides and how your foot feels when it touches the ground. Notice how your weight shifts to your right foot as you bend your left knee and slowly swing your left foot forward.

"If you're not hurrying, you can notice your surroundings while you walk. You can also attend to your breathing. Stay aware of your feet and your rising and falling belly.

"When thoughts or feelings arise, name them 'thought' or 'feeling' and continue walking."

I feel like I am moving in slow motion. In my everyday life, I never think about my weight shifting from side to side or my feet touching the ground as I walk. Not sure what good this does in real life, but whatever. Oh, I'm thinking. I'll name that a "thought."

"Let's pause, take a few mindful breaths and notice how we feel," Veda said.

After a brief pause, Veda said, "I invite you to circle up for a brief discussion on our mats."

We settled in a circle on our mats.

"What came up for you today?" Veda asked.

"The floor movements were relaxing," Lucia said. "They felt like simple movements I could make when I get up in the morning."

"I loved the standing meditation," Simone said. "I sit too much, so this helped get the blood pumping."

"The walking meditation was unusual," I said. "But I'll admit that I felt calm. I hadn't realized all my body does to put one foot in front of the other."

"Thank you for sharing," Veda said. "Let's talk about last week's practice and homework."

"I drank a cup of tea every morning with mindfulness," Lucia said. "And I noticed that Adriana has the most adorable belly laugh."

"I've started to listen to music more mindfully," Simone said.

"Like Yanni?" I asked, with a wink.

"I even listened to a little Yanni for Meghan's sake," Simone said. "Not bad, I have to admit. And I certainly eat chocolate more mindfully. That's holy food, ladies."

Week 3: Mindful Movement

"I noticed that my husband's eyes sparkle when our kids humor him, and I told him that in a handwritten note this morning," I said. "I can hardly believe I said something nice, and it wasn't in a text message! I'm still trying to figure out the best way to integrate the practices into my busy days."

"Thank you for sharing, ladies," Veda said. "This past week I gave my husband a back rub mindfully. I noticed he has a heart-shaped freckle on his left shoulder blade. But I didn't tell him that. I didn't want him to feel self-conscious about it."

"You're killing me with this cuteness," Simone said. "When are we going to get to meet your man? I told the girls that I figured he was meditating in your bedroom the whole time we're here."

Veda laughed.

"Not at all," Veda said. "He's out riding his Harley with his brother Garrett. But, you will get to meet him soon. In fact, he'll be joining us next week."

"A Harley rider in a meditation class?" Simone asked. "I thought I'd seen everything."

"What Simone's trying to say is that we'd love to meet your husband," I said. "Could you two join us for a cookout this evening?"

"Lucia and I will be there with my kids," Simone said, eyes pleading.

"That sounds lovely," Veda said. "I'll talk to my husband and let you know."

Simone pumped her shoulders up one at a time.

"Let's take five minutes to practice writing mindfully," Veda said. "We'll conclude with homework."

Veda passed out our homework, which I quickly reviewed—noting some walking and mindful movement additions. I stuffed it in my purse.

Veda concluded with a blessing.

> *May I be healthy.*
> *May I be balanced.*
> *May I be courageous.*
> *May I be free from suffering and at ease with pain.*
> *May you be healthy.*
> *May you be balanced.*
> *May you be courageous.*
> *May you be free from suffering and at ease with pain.*

"Next week we will practice mindful creations," Veda said. "Lucia, could I speak with you in the kitchen?"

The Cookout

"Is Veda gonna make it?" Simone asked, scooching up to the backyard table with a plate of food.

"Maybe," I said. "She said something about the stars perhaps aligning."

"Sounds about right," Simone said. "Look at our kids, swinging on your jungle gym and being so sweet."

Xavier started shoving his sister too hard on the swing. She nearly fell off the back.

"Xavier! Stop that right now!" Simone called out.

Week 3: Mindful Movement

He stopped and stepped back from the swing, waving at his mom in apology.

"Spoke too soon," I said with a wink.

"What do you think Veda and Lucia were talking about when we walked into class today?" Simone asked.

"I'm not sure," I said. "But I feel like something's going on that they're not telling us."

She nodded.

"Where's Pat?" she asked. "Is he still sulking that Anthony and I aren't together anymore?"

"No, there's a game he wanted to catch, so he's camped out in our living room," I said. "He was the grill master for the meat, so I told him he'd done his duty for the evening."

"These things are the bomb," Simone said, motioning to the skewer in her hand. "I forget, what do you call them?"

"Kabobs," I said.

"Nah," Simone said. "I'm gonna call these 'ka-bombs.' So, are we gonna gang up on Lucia tonight or what?"

The wooden back gate opened. Adriana walked through, a pink sparkly headband adorning her shiny black hair. Lucia followed, shuffling and shoulders drooping.

"Well, look who it is!" Simone announced. "Xavier, Jacqueline, Adriana's here!"

Lucia waved as she walked toward us. She plopped a bag of tortilla chips on the table and a can of salsa.

"I'm ashamed that I didn't bring my famous guacamole," Lucia said, dropping in a chair. "I'm just too tired to make it."

"Well, that's just unacceptable, missy," Simone said, folding her arms. "How do you expect me to pair these ka-bombs with store-bought salsa?"

"Ka-what?" Lucia asked.

"Don't worry about it," I said, grabbing the plate of kabobs, bowl of tangerines and the dish of macaroni and cheese.

I hugged Lucia as I sat the food in front of her. She grabbed a kabob and stared at it.

"Nauseous?" I asked.

"Just not hungry," she said.

"How are you feeling after today?" I asked, grabbing some chips and salsa.

"So tired," Lucia said. "I almost didn't come tonight, but Adriana was dying to see your kids."

"Well, take it easy, hon," I said. I brought an extra chair over, so she could prop up her legs.

"Bella, let your sister have a turn!" I called out.

Bella folded her arms and kept her eyes on the ground as she stomped away.

"Hmm, where does Bella get that arm folding thingy from?" Simone asked me, with a wink.

I rolled my eyes and folded my arms.

"See!" Simone said.

Week 3: Mindful Movement

"I'm a little sore," I confessed.

"Miss I-Run-Five-Miles-for-Fun is sore?" Simone said.

"Yeah, moving slowly is strangely challenging," I said.

"My joints feel a little creaky," Lucia said.

"Speaking of creaky," Simone said. "I hear the gate opening."

"Veda!" Adriana yelled, running to give her a hug.

"I'm glad to see you," Veda said. "You're getting so tall, child."

"And strong," Adriana said. "Watch me go across the monkey bars!"

She darted off and began her trek across the jungle gym.

"Wonderful, darling!" Veda said.

"Good evening, Veda," I said, pulling up a chair for her.

"Where's your hubby?" Simone asked Veda.

"He's a writer, working to get a piece published, and sends his warm regards," she said. "It looks like we have quite an abundance of food."

"Looks like you'll be adding to it," I said, motioning to the cloth bag hanging from her hand.

"I brought us a fermented beverage," she said.

Simone and I raised an eyebrow at one another.

"It's called kombucha," she said. "This is a black tea that I've been fermenting in my pantry for several months."

Veda pulled out the glass canister.

"Uh, what is that white blob floating on top?" Simone asked.

"The SCOBY," Veda said. "An acronym for symbiotic culture of bacteria and yeast."

"Sounds delicious," Simone said, grimacing.

I grabbed some cups.

"Shall we?" I asked.

With the cups filled, we looked at one another and raised our glasses.

"To Lucia's recovery," I said, holding up my favorite ceramic mug, a gift from Lucia.

"To Lucia's discovery," Veda said.

"To Lucia's …" Simone said. "*Re*-discovery. You guys took all the good 'covery' words."

We chuckled.

"Cheers!" Simone said, clinking her cup into Lucia's.

Simone took a sip and gagged.

"Tastes like trash juice," Simone said.

I swallowed and pursed my lips, holding back a cough.

That's one of the worst things I've ever tasted.

Lucia forced a smile.

"I'll admit it's an acquired taste," Veda said. "But it's so healthy for you."

"Well, thank God for that," Simone said.

"I could share my SCOBY if any of you are interested," Veda said.

Week 3: Mindful Movement

"Tempting," Simone said. "But I'll pass."

Simone sat down her glass and looked at her watch.

"I hate to do this, ladies, but I've gotta run," she said, gathering her things. She mouthed, "Sorry," to me.

"I just remembered I need to submit a job application to this organization downtown. The deadline is tomorrow, and I've got a lot to do. But I'll see you gals next Saturday," she said. "Lucia, let me know if you want me to go with you to chemo this week. It's my turn to join you, so don't let Meg weasel her way in."

Lucia nodded.

"My schedule's wide open during the week, as you know," Simone said.

"I hope to hear about your job search during our time next week," Veda said.

"Not much to tell besides sweaty palms and board rooms," she said. "But on the bright side, I bought a new suit and it is cute, ladies. Kids, let's go!"

Xavier and Jacqueline ran to her side.

"See you soon," Simone said, grabbing her kids' hands. "And Lucia, hit me up, girl!"

"Meghan," Lucia said. "Would you go tell Adriana we have ten more minutes before we need to leave?"

When I returned, Lucia thanked me.

"It seems like Adriana is always with you," I said. "I mean, I know she loves hanging with my kids, but shouldn't you be resting and let your sister take care of her?"

"I ... I guess I feel very responsible for Adriana," Lucia said, tiredly. "Maybe it's just how I was raised."

We all looked out at Adriana playing.

"I've always felt very close to her, since the moment she was born," Lucia said. "Did you know Veda was the doula, like a midwife, for Adriana's birth?"

I shook my head, noting an awkward silence.

Lucia looks awful. My resolve to question her is fading. I wish Simone were here to help me.

Veda offered to help clean up.

"Is it OK if I stay here?" Lucia asked.

"Of course, hon," I said.

Veda worked in the kitchen as I walked back out to the backyard for the last load. Lucia was asleep, her head lay on top of her folded arms. Just like she used to do on my kitchen table when she was a school girl. More of her hair was missing.

How much longer will she make it? Who will ever replace my Lucia?

I placed my cardigan over her shoulders. I grabbed our cups and headed back inside. As I crossed the threshold, I stumbled. My favorite mug fell to the floor with a crash. One big piece broke off from its top and shattered.

Week 3: Mindful Movement

Veda looked up as I returned to the kitchen. Since my hands were filled with cups and shards of my broken mug, I attempted to wipe my tears with my left shoulder.

"This mug was a gift from Lucia," I said, holding it up. "It's broken and can't be fixed."

She dried her hands, her eyes filled with sadness. She perked up, remembering something. She held up her right pointer finger for me to wait a moment.

Out of a cloth bag she pulled a blob of brown wrapping tissue. She handed it to me.

"Today, at the farmer's market, something told me to buy this," she said. "I had no idea why, but now I know."

Puzzled, I opened it: a handmade ceramic mug, purple on bottom, beige on top, four brown circles running up the side, like buttons on a sweater.

"I can't fix life's sorrows," she said, gently placing her hand on my forearm. "But I can show you how to listen. Sometimes that's all we can do. And sometimes it makes all the difference."

My heart swelled. A tidal wave of emotions knocked down a wall inside me.

She opened her arms to offer me a hug.

I accepted.

After Veda and Lucia left, I puttered around the kitchen, my mind whirling.

How did Veda know to buy that mug? She can teach me how to listen. But how can I listen? I need quiet to listen. Maybe our spare bedroom would be quiet in the morning. I could give it a try.

Ring. Ring. Ring.

Dad's calling. It's late. I wonder what he wants?

"Hey Dad."

"Hi, honey."

"Everything OK?" I asked.

"Yeah, I was just thinking about you and wanted to see how you're doing," he said.

Truth or dare? I took a breath and heard my heart respond, "Both."

"I'm struggling, Dad," I said. "It's so hard to see Lucia suffer, knowing I can't fix her."

"I know, sweetheart," he said. "But you taking the mindfulness course with her is helping more than you know. When a friend suffers, sometimes all we can offer is our ears, our eyes, our hearts."

"Funny, Veda said something very similar this evening," I said.

"How's it going with Veda?"

"Are you asking if I still think she's kooky?" I said.

"Kinda."

I picked up my new purple mug, felt its ridges and pulled it to my chest.

"Veda is Veda," I said. "I didn't understand what you meant by that before. But now I do."

"I'm glad to hear it, Meg," he said. "She gave you something, didn't she?"

"A mug, after I just broke mine," I said. "Pretty wild."

"She gave you something else, too," he said.

"A Veda hug, yeah," I said. "How'd you know?"

"I just know."

Chapter 6
Week 4: Mindful Creations

If we are not fully ourselves, truly in the present moment,
we miss everything.

—Thich Nhat Hanh

Feeling motivated this morning, I woke up early to sit quietly for five minutes. I followed my quiet time with a quick jog. After my new morning routine, I hopped in my minivan to join the gals at Veda's house for mindfulness practice.

When I knocked on the door, no one answered. *That's weird. And no one's car is here.*

I got back in my minivan to text Simone and saw I'd just missed a text from her.

Simone: How r u? Looking forward to our mindful creations tomorrow. Bringing glitter, just in case!

Tomorrow? What is today? Friday!

With an exasperated sigh, I texted back.

Me: Sitting in front of Veda's house. Thought today was Saturday. Ugh!

Simone: Know what that means?

Me: What?

Simone: Coffee date!

Me: Let me check w Pat. Want to see if Lucia can join us?

Simone: On it.

I entered the coffee shop and saw Simone and Lucia laughing at a table in the corner.

My phone buzzed with a text from Pat: "Kids made it to school on time." I paused to allow myself a moment of gratefulness and reluctantly turned my phone on silent.

"What did I miss?" I asked, as I looked up from my phone.

"The memo that it's Friday!" Simone said, and she and Lucia cracked up.

I rolled my eyes with a smile.

"Glad Pat could spot you today with the kids," Lucia said.

"You and I both," I replied. "I need coffee. Be right back."

I pulled out my new mug from Veda and got it filled to the top with piping hot java.

When I returned to the table, Lucia gave me a sideways glance, the dark circles under her eyes more pronounced than ever.

Week 4: Mindful Creations

"So, what are you going to make for your mindful creation?" Lucia asked, touching her port, a fleshy bump below her collarbone.

"Some sort of writing piece, of course. Not sure what about yet, but definitely writing," I said. "You?"

"A culinary creation," Lucia said with a big smile.

"Ooooh, really?" Simone said. "Whatcha makin'?"

"Tamales," Lucia said. "But not just any tamales. You'll have to wait and see."

"Do you think we'll get to taste them?" I asked.

"I sure hope so," Simone said.

"What about you, Simone?" I asked.

"I'm going to do something with music," Simone said. "You know how my silky smooth voice charms an audience."

"*¡Qué padre!*" Lucia said. "Very cool."

"How do you think the class has been going?" I asked.

"I just love Veda, so it's hard for me to be objective," Lucia said. "As my godmother she's been with me through the most difficult times of my life. But I'm enjoying being with you two and learning how to be more present, which has not been easy lately."

"Same here," I said. "It's special to take part in this class with you two, especially with all we have going on in our lives. The class is helping me slow down and pay attention. I've noticed I actually get more done on the days when I practice sitting meditation for five minutes. I've started setting my alarm ten minutes early, so I can get my full five minutes in.

No one is up at my house, and it's becoming a treasured time for me. I pray for you, Lucia, each morning, and you, too, Simone."

"You're a gem, Meg," Simone said.

"And it sounds like mindfulness is starting to suit you," Lucia said.

"I wouldn't go that far," I said. "I committed to this course, so I figured I might as well give it a good try."

"So you're not convinced yet," Simone said. "Just stubborn. Sounds about right."

After a little laugh, Simone got serious.

"I've gotta be honest with you two. I've felt a little impatient in the classes and haven't done much in the way of the homework practices," Simone admitted. "My mind works about the same speed as my mouth, so—"

She tapped on the right side of her head with her index finger.

"It's a busy little town in here."

Lucia and I snickered.

"I know it's good for me, I'm just struggling to focus because I'm worried about finding a job," Simone said. "Not just any job, but one that is fulfilling and pays the bills. And those bills are piling up."

"I understand," Lucia said.

"Secretly I keep feeling frustrated and guilty because I'm fighting thoughts that mindfulness may not be worth it to me," Simone continued. "I mean, really, besides seeing your two adorable faces, what will I get out of this? We could always just have Saturday morning coffees together. A lot more enjoyable, right?"

WEEK 4: MINDFUL CREATIONS

"All this tells me you're in touch with your thoughts and feelings," Lucia said. "Being present with ourselves doesn't mean it's all calm and joyful inside. Sometimes being present feels silly or pointless to me. But I keep thinking, 'What's the alternative? Living life as an out-of-body, out-of-mind experience, acting happy when I'm really upset? Or being angry about situations that are out of my control?'"

"You're not alone, Simone," I said. "It feels kinda frivolous, a luxury that in real life doesn't seem practical. I've been beating myself up for not feeling like I'm doing and feeling the right things. Or that I'm getting caught up in the woo-woo."

Simone nodded.

"But, Veda told us on the first day that this is *our* practice," I said, "And we can do as much or as little as we want."

"What do you want to get out of the class?" Lucia asked Simone.

"I need wisdom about my job hunt, to make a good decision for me and my kids," Simone said. "I've got an interview today. A new position opened at my previous job, so I'm pretty excited."

"Then set your intention there, Simone," Lucia said. "And decide what you can do in regard to mindfulness practice, even if it feels small."

"I like Meghan's idea of setting the alarm ten minutes early," Simone said. "I love my sleep, but I can part with ten minutes. I'll give it a try this coming week and use those ten minutes to sit or do mindful movement, or perhaps one of the other mindful tricks we'll learn before we're through. When is this class over, anyway?"

"Two more weeks," Lucia said.

"Lucia, how are you?" I asked. "What's the status on your treatment?"

"Chemo is in full swing," she said. "I'm nauseous and super exhausted. This whole mindfulness thing is tough right now, because I don't always want to be present in my sick body and scared mind. I don't know how it's all going to turn out. But I'm grateful for you gals joining me."

She took a sip of coffee.

"I want to be around to celebrate Adriana's *quinceañera*, her fifteenth birthday, when the time comes. I also want to take photos of her on prom night and cheer for her walking across the stage at her college graduation and down the aisle at her wedding. I love her like a daughter, and it rips me open to think of her experiencing life without me."

Simone grabbed tissues from her large silver purse and passed one to me and Lucia.

"And what's even more challenging is that we really can't afford my time out of the office," Lucia said. "I'm grateful for the health benefits at my job; however, I've maxed out my PTO. So Mama picked up another job to try to cover the gap, but it's not enough, and she and I both know it. We eat dinner in silence. Sharing dinner used to be my favorite part of the day, but it's all I can do not to sob during the whole meal. I can't really taste much anyway, thanks to the chemo."

The cappuccino machine sizzled and bubbled behind us.

"Oh, Lucia," I said, gripping my mug. "My heart breaks for you. That's a lot to carry."

"Well, this just won't do," Simone said, folding her arms across her chest.

"What do you mean?" Lucia said.

Week 4: Mindful Creations

"This just won't do," Simone said. "You are going to get your chemo treatments and have enough money to cover everything, even if I have to sell one of my kidneys to pay for it."

"That's sweet, Simone," I said. "But could we find a way to raise money that doesn't involve one of us losing a vital organ?"

"Let's think on that," Simone said. "Listen, I hate to do this, but I've gotta run to prep for my job interview."

"Good luck!" I said.

"Thanks, Meg," Simone asked. "Could I give you a hug, Lucia?"

Lucia rose and Simone hugged her for five breaths.

As Lucia pulled away, her eyes shimmered. "You're beginning to hug like *her*," Lucia said.

Lucia bowed to Simone, wincing as she stood up.

"You don't have to worship me just because I've learned to give magical hugs," Simone said with a wink. "I love you girls. And I'll see you tomorrow. Tomorrow's Saturday, Meghan."

She blew us air kisses and stepped out the coffee shop door.

"I need to leave, too," I said to Lucia. "I'm sorry you are having to deal with all this. I know I've been dragging my feet a bit on learning mindfulness, but that has nothing to do with you. You're like a sister to me, you know that, right?"

She nodded.

"It's an honor to be on this journey with you and Simone," I said. "We will figure out some way to help you. I'll pray … and, um, meditate on it."

"Thank you, Meghan," she said. "See you in the morning."

I ran out the door to catch Simone before she hopped in her car.

"Simone, do you have a sec?"

"For a gorgeous redhead, anytime," she said.

"I've been thinking we should do something fun for Lucia, to get her mind off everything."

"What do you have in mind?"

"What about a sleepover at my parents' house?" I said. "Just like old times."

"Won't your parents enforce a curfew, just like old times?"

"They're out of town this week visiting family," I said.

"So, you're proposing we crash your parents' house while they're gone?" she asked.

I nodded.

"Brilliant," she said.

"I have my moments."

"Welcome, my fellow creators," Veda greeted us.

My coffee is still kicking in, but curiosity is keeping me moving. What does "mindful creations" really mean? I need to write, creatively, today. Who's the darling man sitting beside Veda?

"Mindful creations," Veda said. "Does anyone know what that means?"

Week 4: Mindful Creations

"Heck if I know," Simone said under her breath.

"It means mindful exploring, connecting and practicing our artistic languages, and perhaps trying out new artistic languages. I invite you to stay present with yourself and your art. Use your senses. Smell the pencil lead, touch the chalk and see its dust on your hands, hear the sound of your scissors cutting the paper. Keep in touch with your body movements, as well as thoughts and emotions that may arise.

"Rocks, shells, sprigs and other nature items are here on our entry table, if you'd like some inspiration," Veda continued. "Oh, and you're probably wanting to know who this handsome devil is."

Veda pointed to her husband with a flat, open palm. The tall, tan man had a pile of thick gray hair on his head and blue eyes that matched Veda's.

"This is my husband, George," Veda said. "He's a Harley rider, as you know, but also a poet and visual artist. He'll lead our mindful creation practice today."

We all waved girlishly to George. He was quite good-looking.

"How did you two meet?" Simone asked.

"We met at a poetry reading at the same coffee shop that the four of us met at a few weeks ago," Veda said. "George was back from studying literature in France, and I was back from Italy, where I was exploring art, jewelry and food."

"The air that swept behind us was infused with the scent of fine wine, rich soil and ancient leather tomes," George said.

"Well now, you are a poet, aren't you?" I said.

"He lives and he breathes, the handsome Harley husband with the heart-shaped freckle," Simone said. "I thought you were too good to be true, but here you are."

"Simone!" I exclaimed.

George's eyes grew wide, and his mouth parted as if he were going to say something.

"What?" Simone said. "Oh, I forgot that Veda hadn't told him about the freckle. Could I redeem myself by practicing mindfulness? I'm blushing because I feel embarrassed and sorry. I'll spare you the self-deprecating thoughts running through my head."

"It's quite alright, Simone," Veda said. "And you did a wonderful job practicing mindfulness just now."

Veda continued, "Let's practice sitting meditation."

I feel embarrassed for George, Veda and also Simone. I am blushing. Redheads do that. I'm thinking—"thought." Now come back to the moment, the breath. Breathing in, my belly is expanding. My yoga pants feel a little tight. Breathing out, is it because I ate too much mac 'n cheese this week? Breathing in, yep, yoga pants are definitely tight. Breathing out, I'd better run this evening. Ah, "thought." Breathing in, I feel air in my belly. Breathing out, I feel cool air passing through my lips.

"I invite you to join me on the deck outside the kitchen upstairs," Veda said. "We'll begin our practice of mindful creation. Notice the invitation and join us when you are ready. Be sure to bring your journals with you."

George rang the bell and settled himself beside Veda on the outdoor bench.

Week 4: Mindful Creations

"We will begin with the unending line practice," George said. "Choose a writing instrument from the box beside me. We have pens, pencils, colored pencils, markers and more. In your journal, touch the writing instrument to a blank piece of paper and don't stop moving it until the song I'm playing stops."

I start with circle loops, then go to sideways figure eights, the infinity symbol. Why do I feel strange? Did I not eat enough for breakfast? I must've forgotten my coffee. Nope, I remember drinking coffee out of Pat's "Number One Dad" mug. Maybe the shape I'm drawing is the sign of infinite exhaustion. I look to my right, and Simone's paper is filled with long pink lines up and down the page. To my left Lucia's page is filled with a labyrinth. I bet that's how she feels. I hope she can make it out of this maze she's stuck in right now.

The song ended and George stood up.

"Please stand with me. Visualize your unending line and let your movements replicate the shape of it. For instance, mine is a swirl, starting out small and ending much bigger.

"This is how I will move," George said. "As I move, I do so mindfully, feeling my feet touch the ground, connecting to my art."

He faced us, then turned to his right for a small circle that grew into a bigger and bigger circle the longer he turned.

"You're going to get dizzy," Simone said. "I claim this space over here. We're going to need to spread out a bit."

George turned on the same song.

As the song began, I started with some looping circles, then moved to the infinity eight. Some were bigger than others. Simone was embodying her pink lines in a slow walk back and forth across the deck. Lucia looked like she'd lost her way or had gone mad. She was turning each and every way, seemingly desperate as she turned with military precision again and again. When the song finished, I made one final very tiny infinity eight.

"Inside this blue bin to my left is a plethora of art supplies," Veda said. "You'll find everything from crayons, paint and clay to canvases, art paper, scissors, tape, glue and chalks. Simone, I even put some blank sheets of music paper in there for you, should you want them."

The three of us squatted around the bin, scrounging for what we wanted. I grabbed some light purple art paper, some chalk, dark purple glitter and scissors.

I used white chalk over the purple paper then folded it and began cutting it at random. I opened it to find a round snowflake with the infinity eight in it.

Strange.

I circled the snowflake with sparkle glitter and rounded five of the infinity eights.

My stomach growled.

"Let's gather inside for tea," Veda said.

As we walked in the kitchen, I overheard whispers between Veda and her husband.

"Where is it?" he asked.

"Your left shoulder blade," she said.

"Is that why you always kiss me there?" he asked.

She smiled, looked him in the eyes and kissed him on the lips.

Week 4: Mindful Creations

"Easy, love birds," Simone said.

Inside the kitchen, we sniffed the tea.

"Smells like lavender," Lucia said.

"This is lavender tea," Veda said.

"Tastes like soap," Simone whispered.

I nodded with a grimace.

"Do you have anything to eat?" I asked, sheepishly.

"Sure thing," Veda said. "Let me see what I have."

Just then, someone knocked on the kitchen door.

"Good morning, neighbor," Veda said as she opened the door. She revealed a stunning black woman, likely in her seventies. She wore a royal blue scarf around her head and a matching flowing dress.

"Good morning, ladies," she replied. "And gentleman."

"I brought some benny cake," she said, placing the plate of sesame-seed covered triangles on the table with her wrinkled hands. "It's my husband's favorite. He's traveling, so I'm stress baking because I miss him."

"There sure is a lot of love going around today," Simone said.

I grabbed two and shoved the first one in my mouth.

"Hungry much, Meghan?" Simone asked.

"Starving," I said.

I took a third one and ate it more slowly, mindfully perhaps.

"Mmmm, sweet and nutty," Lucia said, "Just like I remember from my time in Sierra Leone, but a little off due to my taste buds."

"I'm glad you enjoy them."

"You've given me some inspiration for my tamale making this afternoon," Lucia said.

"May I join you?" the neighbor woman asked.

"It's fine with me if it's OK with Veda," Lucia said.

"You are always welcome in my home, friend," Veda said. "Let's transition onto our art creations. Lucia, you can stay here in the kitchen. Simone, I have instruments in the front room, if you'd like them. And, Meghan, you are free to write wherever suits you. I'll be working on my jewelry creation in the basement."

I roamed the house aimlessly. In a spare bedroom I caught a glimpse of Veda's meditation cushion.

Who has time to sit around like that? I have laundry to fold, kids to help with homework. Groceries that need to be bought and put away.

I walked through the hallway to the kitchen, down the stairs to the basement. Veda sat at a round wooden table bending silver wire with two tools in hand. I avoided eye contact, making a swift exit out the basement door.

I should feel happy right now. I'm with two of my best friends at a lovely home. I've been given carte blanche to write whatever I want, wherever I want.

I decided I wanted to write while sitting at the foot of the pine tree.

I sense an uncomfortable amount of freedom. What will I write about? What's the point of writing for fun?

Week 4: Mindful Creations

Circling the tree slowly, I steered clear of putting my face in its prickly coat. I closed my eyes and practiced walking mindfully around it, breathing in its scent. I stepped on a sprig and nearly lost my balance. My hand went into the tree for balance. So much for steering clear of the prickles. My hand touched something cold and smooth. What was that? Against my better judgment, I stuck my face in the tree, carefully, looking for what I might've touched. I saw a small purple glass bottle, three or four inches tall, plugged with a cork. I could see something white inside of it. Paper, maybe? I reached in to grab it, but it was tied to the tree's trunk. I looked around and decided to go for it. Pine needles scratching and thick branches weighing on my head and neck, I uncorked the bottle.

I pulled out a long strip of paper and began reading:

Dear Peter,

I wish you were here with us. I know this tree can't replace you, but we needed it to remind us of you. Of your blue-green eyes, black hair. We'll never get to see you grow up, which is the deepest pain of our hearts, but we will get to see this tree grow. Every morning when I rise, I will see you in this tree. As I water this tree, I will nourish you. I will talk to this tree and send my love to you. To you, out there in the great beyond. Kiss grandma for me.

"It's beautiful, isn't it?"

I was startled. I hadn't heard Veda walk toward me. I lightly crumpled the paper to hide it in my hand, and held my hands behind my back.

"This home belongs to my brother-in-law, Garrett," Veda said. "Many years ago Garrett and his now ex-wife had a son, my nephew, who died unexpectedly when he was very young. They planted this tree in his memory. It was much smaller then. I remember when it was only about three feet tall. It's grown into a stunning tree."

"I am drawn to this tree," I said. "It speaks to me."

"Nature is loquacious if we only listen," she replied. "Take your time listening and writing. When you're finished, please join us inside. We'll be sitting again, then circling up for art sharing and a final discussion."

I spent a few more moments looking up at the tree, then writing my lines of response. I held the note to my heart, then returned the paper to its bottle. It wouldn't fit.

What is keeping the paper from fitting into the bottle?

I pushed back the branches a bit more to see an empty glass orb in the bottom of the bottle. I unfurled the paper a bit to fit around the empty glass circle and re-corked the bottle.

I feel like I've seen that orb before.

Back in the basement, I found my friends practicing their sitting meditation. I tiptoed to my mat and sat on my bolster. I tried to focus on my breathing but struggled to get my mind off the pine tree, the young son and the family that had endured such trauma. I felt nauseous with sadness. I can't imagine losing one of my precious babies. I missed them so much and felt excited to hug them when I got home. Maybe I'd give them one of Veda's magical hugs.

"Please join me in the next room for our circle up," Veda said. "Bring along your art for us to experience."

I laid my writing on the table next to Simone's musical piece. Lucia was coming down the stairs with her tamales. My mouth watered from the sweet, earthy corn aroma.

Week 4: Mindful Creations

"Take a few moments with each piece of art. You may read Meghan's piece and taste Lucia's creation. Simone, would you mind humming your piece?"

"I'll do you one better," Simone said. "I recorded it on my phone. Here you go!"

The piece was strong and energetic, much like Simone. But in the middle it was a little back and forth, confused even. It had a feeling of unsettledness. It ended on a tempered note, mostly resolving but in a complicated, multi-leveled way.

I took a bite of one of Lucia's tamales. Tears came to my eyes. When was the last time I teared up over food?

We all ooh-ed and ahh-ed at the earrings Veda made. Up near the top of the earrings was a wild mess of silver wire, whirled into a quarter-size ball, yet heading down out of the wire was one straight wire, about two inches long, ending in a red freshwater pearl. "The calm after the storm" Veda named them.

The women gathered around my writing, reading silently. They stepped away from the piece, lips pursed and eyes down.

Maybe they don't like it. Well, it's just a first draft. That's OK. I can always revise it.

"That's deep, Meghan," Simone said.

"It's haunting, but in a beautiful sort of way," Lucia said.

"Thank you," I responded. "Simone, your piece is lively and engaging. And Lucia, I am choked up over those tamales. What did you put in those heavenly loaves of corn?"

"I used sesame seeds," Lucia said. "Veda's neighbor inspired me with the benny cakes she brought by this morning."

"Thank you, ladies," Veda said. "I'm moved by your mindful creations. I want to hear about how your mindful practice went today."

"It's the most fun I've had in a long time," Lucia said. "I felt like a child again, free and happy."

Simone hummed a bit.

"Alright, I'm going to step out on a limb here," Simone said. "I told the other girls this yesterday, that I've felt guilty for sitting, and today I felt it again for having fun. I don't really do guilt much, so this is an interesting feeling for me."

"I felt self-conscious about my writing," I said. "I kept worrying it wasn't good enough, I wasn't good enough. And then when I … I learned what I learned today, I felt a lot of love for my family. While we created earlier, I struggled to relax and enjoy it. The to-do list brain was in motion, and I was feeling hungry during most of the practice. I kept having to accept what was coming up and refocus on my glittery snowflake."

"You gonna keep that snowflake?" Simone asked.

"It's yours, lady," I replied.

She smiled broadly.

"I was also preoccupied with fear that my kids are going to get the dreaded cold that's going around," I said. "We're hosting a big cookout soon, and I really don't want to miss it."

"Thank you all for sharing," Veda said, passing out our homework. It included a creation exercise to be done outside.

Week 4: Mindful Creations

"Next week we will practice processing difficult emotions," Veda said.

Veda concluded with a blessing.

> *May you be safe and secure.*
> *May your mind and body be at peace and ease experiencing life's joys and sorrows.*
> *May your spirit be filled with loving kindness.*
> *And may you allow for all things to be just as they are.*

"Would you please arrive early next week?" she asked. "Let's say by 6:45 a.m.?"

A roar of a motorcycle filled the room, then went silent. Someone knocked on the door and opened it. A white man with slicked back salt-and-pepper hair and a thick beard stuck his head in.

"Hi, Garrett," Veda said.

"I'm here to see Lucia," he said, opening the door to reveal his tall, muscular frame. "Am I interrupting?"

"Not at all," Veda said. "We're concluding our session."

Garrett draped his leather jacket over his shoulder, holding it by his pointer finger.

"I've got to leave to pick up Adriana from school," Lucia said, frantically packing her things. "She has art club today and asked me to get her when it was over."

"Be well, Lucia," Veda said, opening her arms and giving her a long hug.

Simone stared at the visitor, from his chiseled jaw and tattooed forearms to his leather boots.

"Who is that handsome man in leather?" Simone asked, a little too loudly.

"Garrett, Veda's brother-in-law," I whispered.

"Well that's unfortunate," Simone said. "I cannot resist a man on a motorcycle. How old do you think he is?"

"I'd peg him around forty-two or forty-three," I said.

"Only about eight years older than me," she said, pumping her eyebrows.

"Did you invite Lucia to our sleepover tonight?" I asked.

"Yes, she's in," Simone said. "I'll pick you two up at five o'clock. Oh, and I've got dinner covered."

Lucia released Veda's hug, then joined Garrett outside, where they exchanged a few muffled words before Lucia drove away.

Simone and I stayed and brought Veda up to speed on Lucia's situation. We discussed how we might be able to help Lucia, especially financially.

"Let me meditate on this," Veda said, catching her husband's eye. "I'll see you next week for a practice in handling difficult emotions. Seems like we may have enough of these to practice well."

"Meghan, may I speak with you?" George said.

"Sure," I replied.

"I'll catch you next week, Veda," Simone said. "Meghan, I'll see you tonight. And, if you confuse Friday for Saturday again next week, I'll see you at the coffee shop. That caramel macchiato was to die for."

"You have a strong voice, Meghan," George said. "Might you consider enrolling in an MFA program?"

"I've considered it," I said. "You think I have what it takes?"

"I do," he said. "I've read several of your articles. Here's my card if you decide to pursue it. I'd be happy to write you a recommendation."

I floated out to my minivan.

Might this be my next step? Can I do this and run a business? My stomach growled. I'd better address first things first: lunch. What will I make? In this moment I choose to breathe slowly, noticing that I feel the urge to launch into planning mode.

I put my minivan in reverse and passed the special pine tree as I left Veda's driveway. I shuddered.

All I could think about was how I couldn't wait to hug my kids when I got home.

The Sleepover

"I feel so deviant," Simone whispered, as I unlocked my parents' front door.

"They know we're spending the night, you know that, right?" I said.

"You're killing the rebellious vibe, Meg," Simone said, flicking my ponytail. "Lucia, could you grab my three bags?"

Lucia's eyes grew wide. Simone winked at Lucia and headed back to her car.

Lucia looked around the home quietly, running her fingers along the dining room table and heading toward the bedroom.

"You still have my bed here," she said.

"Always," I said, putting my arm around her. "I think you spent more nights here than your own house."

She flinched and I removed my arm.

"Dinner is served!" Simone said, presenting the pan. "Lucia's favorite, *tres leches* cake. I baked it myself."

"Umm, that's dessert," I said.

"No parents, no kids, no rules, ladies," Simone said.

She grabbed three forks and we sat down at the dining room table to eat.

"The texture is great, Simone," Lucia said.

"Is that your way of saying it tastes gross?" Simone asked.

"Not at all, I just can't taste much," she said. "But the texture is outstanding."

"It's delicious, Simone," I said. "Maybe we can enjoy the dessert in silence, like we've learned in class."

In the tres leches, *three milks cake, I noted the moist sweet bread complemented by a hint of cinnamon.*

"You know we're going to need to order some pizza, right?" I said, grabbing my phone. "Half cheese, half red pepper and onion?"

Week 4: Mindful Creations

They nodded while I placed the order.

"Pizza will be here in a half hour," I said.

Lucia excused herself to use the restroom.

Simone and I grabbed some games.

"Three-player checkers?" Simone asked.

"Absolutely," I responded.

"You know we're just going to play two truths and a lie," Simone said.

"Uh, Meghan," Lucia called from the restroom. "Would you please come here?"

I half jogged to the restroom door and knocked.

"Come in."

"What's wrong?" I asked.

"The toilet is running, and it won't stop," she said, running her fingers through her hair. She threw a patch of hair in the toilet.

I jiggled the handle.

"I have to flush twice since I'm in chemo," she said. "I must've gotten impatient."

She walked to the mirror. I caught a glimpse of Simone in the doorway.

"Meg, I'm losing my hair," she said, tilting her head around to see the bald spots.

Simone barged in. "You are beautiful, Lucy Lou."

"That's kind of you, but I think it's time," Lucia said.

"Time for what?" I asked.

"To shave it off," Lucia said.

I stopped breathing.

"Are you sure?" Simone asked.

She nodded.

"Well, by the strong scent of Brut in this small bathroom … ," Simone said. "I'd guess that Meg's dad has some clippers nearby."

She rustled in the cabinet under the sink.

"Ah ha!" she said, holding up the clippers.

In silence we set up a chair in front of the bathroom mirror, pinned a towel around Lucia's neck and plugged in the clippers.

"Are you completely sure?" I asked, placing my hands on her shoulders.

She nodded again, placing a short guard on the clippers and handing it to me.

I cleared my throat as I felt my eyes burn.

This is what Lucia wants. And tonight is all about Lucia.

Simone grabbed Lucia's hand. Lucia's jaw was set, her face determined.

With a deep breath, I slowly mowed the first pass just above her right ear. Her shiny black hair fell on my bare feet.

I checked Lucia's face through my blurred vision. She sat straight with sad, resolute eyes.

I made the second pass just as slowly. Simone wiped her eyes with her free hand.

Week 4: Mindful Creations

Gripped by the urge to rush each pass, I breathed in before each row, out as I shaved.

If I can be fully present for this, I can be present for anything.

With her hair shaved completely, I looked Lucia in the eyes, then kissed her forehead.

As we swept up the floor, the doorbell rang.

"Pizza's here," I said. "I'll get it."

I sat the pizza on the dining room table.

"Let's eat, ladies," I called, feeling exhaustion sweep over me. "It's hot."

I heard the clippers buzzing and walked back to the bathroom.

I opened the door. "Did I miss a spot, Lucia?" I asked.

But it wasn't Lucia in the chair. It was Simone.

She was shaving a line down the center of her thick, curly hair.

"Simone!" I cried, catching a glimpse of Lucia's gaping stare.

"I can't let Lucia run around getting all the sympathy looks alone," Simone said. "Plus, these eyes of mine have been waiting for their chance to shine my whole life."

Lucia's eyes lit up as she smiled and shook her head at Simone.

"Let's collect it," I said.

"Collect *what*?" Simone asked.

"Your hair, to donate," I said, running to grab a plastic bag.

Lucia tied Simone's hair in pigtails and cut them off into the bag. Then I shaved what was left.

"The pizza's getting cold," Simone said, heading to the door.

I sat down in the chair. She shot me a look.

"Hand it here," I said, opening my left hand, palm up.

Simone smiled and gave me the clippers. "My pleasure, darlin'."

Lucia cut my ponytail, with a tear running down her face. She held the handful of hair to her chest. I shaved off the rest of my red locks one row at a time.

Wow, I look really pale without my hair. I wonder what Pat will think.

Simone and Lucia hugged me.

"You know Pat's going to kill you," Simone said, releasing her hug.

I smiled.

We stood in front of the mirror, arms around one another's waists, heads buzzed.

"Wrap us in some robes and you could call us the three monkskateers," Simone said, rubbing our heads. "Now let's eat that pizza!"

Chapter 7
Week 5: Tools to Process Difficult Emotions

You are the sky. Everything else—it's just the weather.
—Pema Chödrön

I woke up with a sore throat.

I knew I was going to get that cold that's been going around my kids' school. I don't have time to be sick.

I managed to get myself out of bed and to our mindfulness class on time. It was still dark when I pulled into Veda's driveway. I popped a cough drop in my mouth and headed into the basement.

No one was in the basement.

"Hello?" I said, rubbing my buzzed hair. *Still feels weird.*

I swear if I got the day wrong again I'm going to have a hissy fit right here in Veda's basement. I'll kill all the Zen vibes, and I'll feel bad about it.

"Meghan," I heard a muffled chorus of women calling my name.

Where are they? It doesn't sound like it's coming from inside.

I stepped outdoors and heard the chorus again. I looked up to see Veda, Lucia and Simone perched on the porch of the extravagant treehouse, a bright outdoor light shining behind them. I climbed the flights of stairs to arrive on the treehouse porch.

"Welcome to my swanky new apartment," Simone said with a smile. "Did you see that there's carpet and a TV and a ceiling fan? Seriously, I can fit a bed in here. Can you imagine how quiet it must be up here at night?"

"Yeah, no kids, no phone," I said.

"Oh, there's a phone in there, don't worry about that," Simone said.

"Good morning, Meghan," Veda said.

"Good morning, or is it morning?" I said, stretching my arms in the air with a yawn.

"It looks like a communal mindful assignment was completed last week?"

She looked at the tops of our heads and smiled.

"Meghan told me she was breathing mindfully while she shaved our heads," Simone said. "But I'd call it more of a hyperventilation."

"How beautiful you all are," Veda said, her eyes glistening. "Lucia is truly blessed to have you as her friends. And I am honored to join you on this sojourn.

"You may be wondering why I asked you to arrive while it's still dark," Veda said, moving into the treehouse.

As we sat on the floor, Veda shared the purpose of our day.

Week 5: Tools to Process Difficult Emotions

"Today we'll be practicing ways to handle difficult emotions," Veda said. "Perhaps you've already experienced some unpleasant events this morning."

"Like fighting with my kids to get up while it was still dark," Simone said.

"Or seeing Mama asleep in the living room chair," Lucia said, "Where she sleeps when she's worried."

"Or waking up with the sore throat that I feared," I said.

"Exactly," Veda said. "You see, one of the greatest gifts we can give ourselves is learning to see what happens in life as always changing. We can choose not to thrash against it or claim it as ourselves, but simply recognize what's going on and allow it to pass, as all things do."

"One thing Papa used to tell me was 'If you don't like the way something is going, don't worry, it will change,'" Lucia said. "'And if you do like the way something is going, enjoy it, it will change, too.'"

"What a poignant concept," Veda said. "That's exactly why we're here this morning."

"Let me get this straight," Simone said. "We're hanging out in a treehouse that should be named a penthouse to discuss the changing nature of everything? Sounds like a recipe for a freak-out session."

"Something like that," Veda said. "We're practicing equanimity."

"What's equanimity?" Lucia asked.

"Equanimity is being able to recognize the various elements of our experiences with a whole heart, calm body and open mind," Veda said. "It's holding space for peace and calmness in the midst of the chaos of life."

Oh boy, here comes the woo-woo.

"Like meditating," Lucia said.

"Yes, we are looking life in the face, accepting what's there and ceasing to struggle," Veda said. "You can find freedom no matter what life brings your way."

"And how do we do that?" I asked.

"First, we identify the emotion we're feeling, such as anger, fear or sadness," Veda said. "We also listen to thoughts we may be having and physical sensations we may be feeling. Then we let it be as it is. We infuse the situation with compassion. We investigate the roots of our feelings and detach from the thoughts, emotions and sensations."

"Yeah, but aren't we supposed to be intimate with what's going on?" I asked. "How do we at the same time be intimate and detach?"

"I know this can be a challenging concept," Veda said. "It's one I struggled with for a long time. We recognize that our thoughts, emotions and body sensations are just that—thoughts, emotions and body sensations. We don't identify with them as being us, just realize we are experiencing them, like a passing cloud."

"A passing cloud," I said. "That may take a minute to sink in."

"While you let it sink in, Mother Nature is preparing our demonstration," Veda said. "The *real* reason you are all here at such an early hour. Please join me on the treehouse porch, and let's watch the show in silence."

As we stepped onto the porch, the navy-blue sky awaited us. Within a few moments, a lightening of blue began at the bottom. A giant, radiant eye began to open. Blues transformed to radiant pinks and oranges. Rays of light beamed through misty-gray clouds, backlighting the deceased son's pine tree. After several minutes had passed, the full golden circle hung, blazing above the horizon.

I looked over at Simone. Her beautiful deep brown skin shined with health as she pursed her red lips. Her buzzed hair was quite becoming as her lively brown eyes watched the sun rise. Lucia's eyes were closed as the warm light illuminated her tan skin. Veda's bright blue eyes were gliding gracefully over the sky's scene.

Veda invited us back into the treehouse.

"What came up for you as you watched the sunrise?" she asked.

"You picked a beautiful morning for watching the sunrise," Simone said. "Wait, is it always beautiful like that?"

We laughed.

"I felt a mix of calmness and restlessness," I said. "It's tough for me to stay fully present without getting antsy, always feeling like I need to be doing something. But it was quite a show this morning."

"I practiced letting the sky change without trying to change it or anticipate its next move, as crazy as that seems," Lucia said.

"That's equanimity," Veda said. "The sky represents our experiences. We see the sky change colors, clouds come and go, and the sun moves up into the sky, just like we can see our experiences come and go, morph and move, and explore it without attaching to an outcome. We practice being non-judgmental explorers."

I bit my lip.

"The sun provides a powerful reminder," Veda said. "A reminder to glow."

"What do you mean by 'glow'?" Lucia asked.

"Glow, actually GLOWY, is an acronym I use in my daily practice," she said. "I've added this practice to your weekly homework. G stands for 'grateful.' I remember things that are a blessing. L is for 'lift up,' for the things that need prayer. O is for 'observe' to remind me to pay attention to what I notice in my mind, body and soul. W stands for 'wholesome intention,' what I intend for my day. Y is for 'you are,' the beginning of a positive affirmation, to send me out into my day."

Veda invited us to practice a GLOWY reflection:

G: *I'm grateful for watching a beautiful sunrise with my friends.*

L: *I lift up Lucia; may she heal and find peace.*

O: *I notice that I feel fairly calm ... and sick.*

W: *My wholesome intention is to be present for our time together today.*

Y: *You are a good friend with a beautiful, adventuresome soul.*

"Let's head to the basement for some sitting practice," Veda said. "I invite you to feel your feet touch the stairs on your way down."

After a long sitting session, we gathered in a circle on the floor. Veda handed us a sheet of paper.

"I want you to write one example of an unpleasant event, one example of a pleasant event and one neutral happening from this past week," she said.

I cleared my throat and felt a dull ache as I swallowed. I touched my pen to my paper and took a deep breath.

Let's start with the unpleasant: I'm sick and don't have time to be sick. My throat hurts to swallow, my lymph nodes ache and my ears are starting to plug up. I feel angry that I have to deal with sickness and risk letting my family and clients down. I'm also worried that my whole family will come down with a cold and miss days of school and work. Alright, that's enough unpleasant.

What happened that was pleasant? We spent all day Sunday at home as a family. We played games and popped popcorn. We even went for a bike ride to the park. The fresh air felt amazing. I felt free and happy on my bike, gliding along the trail with my family all together. Pat told me I looked beautiful with short hair. I think so, too.

Now, what was neutral this week? What does that even look like? Maybe doing dishes was neutral? I didn't feel one way or another about it. I just washed the dishes.

"When we encounter a situation, good, bad or neutral, we have a choice about how we respond," Veda said. "And one way we can invite wisdom into our responses is by giving some space between the situation and our response, to give ourselves time to be aware of the external condition and our internal environment.

"There's another great acronym that helps guide us through our life encounters," Veda said. "It's R-A-I-N. R.A.I.N. is an acronym that was coined long ago by Michele McDonald, a meditation teacher.

"R stands for 'recognize what's going on.' What are your thoughts and feelings? How is your body responding—is your jaw clenched, are your eyebrows furrowed, do you feel your stomach flipping?

"A stands for 'allowing,' letting the situation be what it is without trying to change it.

"I is for 'investigating.' We are exploring the roots of our pain, happiness or other emotion. Perhaps we're reacting based on a habitual pattern.

"N is for 'not identifying with our thoughts, feelings and body sensations.' Like we discussed earlier—let thoughts be thoughts, feelings be feelings and body sensations be body sensations. None of these are you."

"May I share something I find interesting, Veda?" Lucia asked.

"Of course."

"In Spanish we use two different verbs to communicate permanent or temporary states of 'I am,'" Lucia said. "*Soy* is used for permanent or lasting attributes. Like, '*Soy Lucia.*' I'm Lucia. However, we use *estoy* when talking about temporary conditions, like emotions. Such as '*Estoy enojada,*' 'I'm mad.'"

"How interesting," I said. "So, *estoy* tips a proverbial hat at the temporary, changing nature of emotions, and *soy* is unchanging. What a useful distinction. I wish English had a verb form like that. It might help us attach less to our emotions."

"This sounds great, but it's tough to calm down in the moment," Simone said. "Sometimes people, as well as small children who share my DNA and last name, get under my skin, and I want to give them a piece of my mind."

"By training with R.A.I.N., we can bring awareness to our habits," Veda said. "By giving space before responding, we open up all kinds of options while we honor our own experience with compassion and understanding. R.A.I.N. helps keep events in perspective and allows us to cultivate inner calm, even when people push our buttons."

"I actually think the acronym should be B.R.A.I.N.," I said. "We should first breathe to give space."

Week 5: Tools to Process Difficult Emotions

"I like that, Meghan," Veda said. "Our breath grounds us in the moment and in our bodies. I may use that acronym moving forward."

"Leave it to the writer to come up with a new acronym," Simone said, winking at me.

"Speaking of writing, let's take fifteen minutes to write," Veda said. "I encourage you to write stream of consciousness."

I wrote of more frustration with my cold and the queasiness I'd been experiencing, but then went off in a completely different direction. I was feeling frustrated with a conversation I had with Pat this past week. He continued working very long hours and even after several discussions, we were struggling to eat dinner as a family. A task list broke out and my hand began cramping.

Maybe I shield myself from insecurity by doing-doing-doing. I try to prove my value by working myself to the nub, both in my personal and professional life. A client asks for content the next morning and can I work through the night to draft it? I'm on it. What's that all about? A trip to the other side of the world would give me space to breathe. Breathing: that's the first step to dealing with frustration, right?

I looked up to see Veda setting a small wooden mannequin in front of me, like the kind you'd see in artist studios.

"Now that you've completed your sitting and writing meditations, I invite you to draw your thoughts, feelings and sensations on your mannequins. You may use the markers, pens and paints here in the art bin. You'll have fifteen minutes, and more if you need it."

The phone rang, and Veda left the room to answer it.

"Lucia," Veda said. "You have a phone call."

"I didn't realize people still had landlines," Simone said. "I'm not sure I know a single phone number by heart."

"Yeah, I think I only know two," I said. "My grandparents' and my husband's."

I grabbed some markers and paints and sat down, staring at my wooden figurine. I drew a blue swirl on its forehead. I painted the hands fire orange. I painted the neck red. I drew a circle on the stomach, filled it with white and gray. I drew black dots down the spine like bullet points. I painted a red line along the tops of the shoulders, then tried to relax my own shoulders.

I looked over at Simone's mannequin. She drew a red swirl on the top of the head and a black maze across the chest. Blue pants were painted on the mannequin. The arms of the figure were in an "I don't know" position: arms up at ninety degrees and palms facing the ceiling.

Lucia walked back in the room, head down and breathing loudly. She grabbed some art supplies and sat, staring at the mannequin clenched in her left hand.

"Everything OK?" Simone asked.

"It was my mama on the phone," Lucia said. "She keeps calling wherever I am—work, friends' houses, here. I'm struggling to fight for my life and have her worry heaped on top of it."

"I know she must be worried," Simone said. "But it is a lot for you to carry."

Lucia nodded slightly, then returned her gaze to her captive figurine. She used her hands and spread brown paint all over the mannequin in a

Week 5: Tools to Process Difficult Emotions

messy fashion. Then she smeared a thick red line horizontally across the breast.

Simone and I stared at the mannequin, then at each other.

"Please join me upstairs for tea," Veda called down the stairs. "Bring along your journals."

We ascended the stairs in silence.

Veda poured the tea and handed us each a mug.

"For the next fifteen minutes you're invited to mindfully drink your tea and reflect on today's experiences in your journal," Veda said. "After this silent reflection time, we'll circle up to share our artwork and experiences from today's practice."

Lucia took a deep breath in and a long, measured breath out. She began scrawling furiously.

I lifted the tea to my nose and smelled warm, sweet bread.

I bet this is the Pu-erh tea Veda loves. It tastes so earthy. One of these days, I hope Veda serves coffee. Just once.

I tentatively began writing, noting how I felt uncomfortable with Lucia's discomfort. I forced myself to reflect on the day: *The pink and orange sunrise drifts through my mind, along with the pine tree. My sitting practice feels better today. I notice my thoughts and feelings, then gently bring my mind back to my breath. The mannequin art was interesting. My hands looked like they were on fire, like my shoulders. And my poor backbone, riddled with a tattooed to-do list. But Lucia's broke my heart. I'm worried about her. She's always so even-keeled, but she seems like she's on the verge of cracking. I wonder if we can pull off a fundraiser. Or if Veda has another idea.*

Ding, ding, ding.

In the basement, we sat our mannequins on the table and observed their nuances in silence. Veda placed a piece of paper beside each one on which we gave our thoughts. I commented on Simone's mannequin: "Is it true you don't know? Surrender to the swirl and see where the maze leads you." All I could think to write on Lucia's paper was "I'm sorry."

Simone commented on my paper that I might consider cooling off doing so much work. Lucia said she connected with the swirling blue on my forehead, spinning without an end in sight. Veda commented, asking where purple lived in my body.

"Let's circle up," Veda said. "Before we begin, I want to remind you that we have next week off due to spring break. The week after that is our day of silence. I'll be emailing further details on the day of silence."

She handed out our homework. I noted that she'd added journaling about unpleasant, pleasant and neutral events.

I like the GLOWY practice. It's easy to remember. Even if it's the only thing I do this week.

"Would anyone like to share what came up today?"

"Fear about not finding a job and the risk of losing my home," Simone said. "I have a second interview with my old job next week. It's getting serious, so I'm hopeful."

"The usual frustrations," I said, coughing. "Spouse struggles, work issues, me issues, this blasted cold issue."

"Would you like to share, Lucia?" Veda said.

"I'm angry," she spouted. "I'm angry I have cancer, I'm angry I can't make my mama relax, I'm angry I don't have enough money to manage my sickness, and that work, my one oasis, is getting weird. It's like no one knows what to do with me. I just need a hug and for someone to tell me it's all going to be OK. But it might not be OK and that makes me feel very turbulent inside."

We all looked at her with concerned eyes.

"I need to go," Lucia said, standing abruptly.

"Is there anything we can do?" I asked.

"No," she said. "I just need to be alone. If my mama calls, tell her I'm out on a walk."

We watched Lucia exit the basement door. Veda followed her and spoke to her for a moment outside the door. Veda returned to the table.

"What are we going to do?" I asked.

"I've been thinking about your suggestion, the fundraiser," Veda said. "I have an idea."

Ring, ring, ring.

Ugh, if one more person calls me today, I'm going to scream. Can't a girl take a sick day once a year? I may have to learn the fine art of putting my phone on silent.

I turned my phone over. Simone. Again.

I'll let her leave a voicemail.

I scrolled through my notifications. Simone had called three times today. And texted six.

Simone: Hey, Meg. Call me when u get a sec.

Simone: I need to talk w u sometime this morning.

Simone: Possible to call me over lunch?

Simone: You down with that cold? Need me to come over? At least then I'd get to talk to you.

Simone: Would 2pm work?

Simone: Please call me ASAP!!!

Now a new text from Pat: "You need to call Simone right now."

Alright, already. I'll call Simone.

Ring.

"Meg, I thought you'd never call."

I sneezed.

"What's so urgent you had to wake a sick girl?" I asked.

"Have you talked to Veda?" she asked.

"No, what's wrong?"

"It's Lucia. She's missing."

I pulled into Veda's driveway. I didn't see any other vehicles. I got out of my minivan.

Where is Lucia? What if she's in a ditch somewhere? With no one to help her out. Her mom must be freaked out.

I began pacing for several minutes.

Week 5: Tools to Process Difficult Emotions

Veda's station wagon pulled into the driveway. She and Simone stepped out.

"Where have you been?" I asked as they walked toward me.

"I could've asked you the same question for the last seven hours," Simone said.

"Sorry," I said, blowing my nose.

"There's no time to fight," Simone said. "We need to find Lucy Lou."

"She's not at work, the coffee shop or her sister's house," Veda said.

"And obviously not at home," Simone said, checking her phone.

"We've called the police," Veda said. "We've also alerted her doctor, your dad and Cora."

"We could drive around," I said.

"We've been doing that since 8 a.m., shortly after Lucia's mom called," Simone said. "I could hardly understand a word she said because she was so hysterical."

"So, she's been missing since yesterday afternoon," I said. "It seems odd she never went home after our session. And didn't call anyone. It's almost like she didn't want anyone to find her."

"Or she's in a ditch," Simone said.

"Don't say that," I replied. "What should we do?"

"Let's check in with ourselves for just a moment," Veda said, closing her eyes.

We're checking in now? Seriously? How can I check in when Lucia is missing?

"Breathing in, I notice anxiety and fear," Veda said. "Breathing out, I release anxiety and fear."

She opened her eyes. Somehow I felt a little better.

"I see three choices," Simone said. "Stress eat double chocolate fudge ice cream, breathe with fake calmness or make some rockin' plans to help Lucia with Veda's ingenious fundraiser idea."

"Who says we can't do all three?" I asked.

"Now that's my girl!" Simone said.

We entered the brick university building, where we'd met during the mindfulness introduction session. Simone began turning on the lights and pushing back the pocket doors of the three adjoining spaces.

"What time does it begin?" I asked.

"Six o'clock," Simone said.

"And we have enough people to fill all the slots?" I asked.

"Yes," Simone said. "I did have to recruit my two kids, mother and my ex-husband, but yes, we've got it covered."

She turned on the lights to reveal several connected rooms filled with glittered streamers and sparkling tablecloths. I saw my dark purple glitter snowflake hanging above the table of honor.

Simone caught me gawking.

"You know what they say," Simone said. "It ain't a thing …"

"Unless it's got some bling!" I said, chuckling.

Week 5: Tools to Process Difficult Emotions

Veda brought over some homemade lasagna and salad.

"I figured we should have one last good meal before this twenty-four-hour marathon begins," Veda said.

"Is the track cleared off and the mats set up and the water station prepped?" I asked.

"Yes, task master," Simone said. "Still no word from Lucia?"

"No, she hasn't returned any of my calls or texts since our last class," I replied. After taking a bite of my lasagna, I asked, "Have you heard from her?"

"Not once in the last week," Simone said, stabbing her salad.

Veda checked her cell phone.

"I missed a call from Lucia's mom," Veda said. "I'll be right back."

When we finished our dinner, Veda returned.

"What'd Lucia's mom want?" I asked.

"Lucia's still not been found," Veda said. "Her mom asked that we call off the event."

"What?" Simone said. "Why?"

"She said that without Lucia, the fundraiser is of no use."

Veda looked off at a distance.

"Lucia just needs time," she said. "Let's honor her space."

"So, yes or no to the event?" Simone asked.

"Let's stick with our plan," Veda said. "You never know what might happen."

The Chaos Antidote

"Here are the first participants," Simone said.

Simone opened the front door.

"Welcome to the Meditation-a-Thon!" she said.

Simone showed the participants around the grounds: the sitting meditation cushions, the mindful movement mats, the indoor walking track, the journaling and art station and the tea-making space.

Simone manned the tea space, greeting her excited first guest.

"Wait, we get to drink tea and journal as part of our time slot?" the college student asked. "That's so cool."

A little boy came through the door and went straight for the art table, dragging his mom, dad and sister behind him. I oversaw the journal and art station.

Veda led the sitting, walking and movement areas. She greeted a few middle-aged couples, who stretched as they waited to begin.

Simone moved to the microphone.

"Thank you for joining us for the Meditation-a-Thon," Simone said. "As you know, our dear friend Lucia Gonzalez has been diagnosed with breast cancer. Your meditation time, sponsored by your support and your loved ones' support, will help Lucia get the treatment she needs to fight this cancer. Donations will be accepted through the end of next week.

"First things first, you're here to meditate, but what is meditation? Meditation is the practice of being mindful—being aware of what's going on inside and around us. 'Being with what is,' as a friend once told me. Now, let's kick off our first hour of our twenty-four-hour Meditation-a-Thon. You are free to spend your time sitting, moving on the mats, walking on the track, journaling and creating visual art or making and

Week 5: Tools to Process Difficult Emotions

enjoying tea. We'll be on hand to provide some guidance on mindfulness. We'll start with an instrumental song. Please get comfortable and really listen to the music. And who said being mindful isn't fun?"

I heard "Morning Light" by Yanni begin. I laughed and shook my head at Simone. She smiled widely.

We helped guide the participants as they moved and sat, drew and wrote. I saw a middle-school-aged girl walking the indoor track.

I helped the little boy and his family trace their outlines on paper and decorate them.

The phone rang. Simone's eyes darted to mine. "Lucia's mom?" she lipped to me. I shrugged with a grimace and jogged to the phone. It was a participant asking for directions.

Another group entered just before 7 p.m.: Simone's mom, kids and ex-husband, Anthony. And Adriana.

Adriana stood with slumped shoulders, pushing back her cuticles.

"Adriana's grandma called and asked that we bring her," Anthony said. "Is Lucia here?"

"Not yet," Simone said. "Let's try out the walking track."

"Any further word from Lucia's Mom?" I asked Veda.

"Nothing yet," she replied.

Adriana dragged her feet, walking head-down toward the kitchen. I joined her.

"Hey, kiddo," I said. "Can I get you something to eat?"

"No," she said, her shoulders beginning to shake.

"Oh, Adriana," I said. "It's going to be OK."

"No, it's not!" she shouted.

I shut the kitchen door and dropped one knee to the floor, so I could be on eye level with her.

"We can't find Aunt Lucia," she said. "And she's sick."

It feels unfair that an eight-year-old must bear this heartbreak.

"I know, sweetie," I said, pulling a tissue from my pocket to wipe her face.

She really does have beautiful hazel eyes.

"What am I going to do without her?" she said. "She's like a mom to me."

Simone popped her head in the door.

"Lucia's mom is here," she said. "You're gonna need to keep an eye on Adriana. It's gettin' real out here."

I peeked out the door. Lucia's mom was hysterical. Veda took her to the back and spoke with her.

I steered Adriana to the kitchen table and grabbed us some crackers. We ate in silence. The crackers tasted bitter.

A knock on the door, and Cora, Veda's sister, entered.

"I heard Adriana was in here," Cora said, opening her arms.

Adriana ran and hugged Cora's waist, almost knocking her over. I smoothed Adriana's glossy dark hair and excused myself.

Week 5: Tools to Process Difficult Emotions

When Lucia's mom had calmed a bit, Veda asked us to walk her through the stations. She kneeled during the sitting meditation and asked for a candle to light. Simone brought out a palo santo-scented candle, a gift from Veda.

At midnight, we began working in shifts. Veda led the midnight to 2 a.m. shift. I oversaw the 2 a.m. to 4 a.m. slot, and Simone finished the night until 6 a.m. At 6 a.m. we gathered on the upper deck with the participants to watch the sunrise. When the sun was up, Veda explained the changing of life, the movement of our thoughts and feelings. Subdued, the participants gathered at the art table and painted the sunrise.

"I need food," I said.

"You're in luck," Simone said. "Look in the fridge."

I pulled out an egg casserole and chocolate banana muffins.

"Simone, you're the best," I said.

"Don't thank me, thank Lucia's mom," she said.

"I hope she got some sleep last night," I said. "Any word on Lucia?"

"Nothing," Veda said. "I kept thinking that she'd show up."

"Like when I smelled the breakfast?"

We spun around to see Lucia in the doorway. She looked exhausted, her clothes rumpled.

"Lucia!" I cried.

We ran to envelop her in a group hug.

"Are you OK?" I asked. "Where have you been? Does your mom know you're here?"

"I'll answer all your questions," Lucia said. "But I need some of my mama's casserole and muffins. It smells like home."

Simone helped the participants keep practicing their walking and sitting while Veda and I prepped breakfast. Lucia sat at the kitchen table, quietly staring out the window.

Simone returned and we joined hands.

"I'm so grateful you've returned," Veda said.

"I'm thankful you're OK," I said.

"I appreciate that you were on time for breakfast," Simone said, with a wink. "But seriously, I'm grateful to have you back with us, Lucia."

We began eating, and Simone stopped, put down her utensils and stared at Lucia.

"Now, I'm happy you're back, but you've got some explaining to do," Simone said. "Where've you been? We've been worried sick about you. And don't even get us started on your mama."

"I'm sorry I disappeared like that," Lucia said. "I felt overwhelmed with the feelings exploding inside of me. I felt it was best to just be alone and sit with what I was experiencing."

"So you were trying to get a head start on the day of silence?" Simone said, shaking her head. "Well, you could've told us."

"I considered telling you all, Mama even," Lucia said. "But I didn't want anyone to feel sorry for me, or to interrupt what I needed to do."

"What did you need to do?" I asked.

"Sit in silence."

Week 5: Tools to Process Difficult Emotions

"What'd you learn up there, Lucia?" Veda asked.

"I learned to quit fighting," Lucia said.

We gasped.

"Not quit fighting, as in give up on living," Lucia said. "I mean quit fighting the reality of my life. I have breast cancer. I can't afford to not get paid at work while I get treatments and stay home sick. Mama is beside herself with worry. Papa can't placate her. I don't have a significant other or a house of my own. But, I do have a job that I love. I still have breath in my lungs. And I have the best friends a girl could ask for. I love you, *chicas*."

Simone passed around the box of tissues.

"We love you too, Lucy Lou," Simone said.

"Lucia, I'm grateful you're safe, and it sounds like you had quite the experience," I said. "But the journalist in me feels the burn of the million-dollar question: where have you been for the last week?"

Lucia looked sheepishly at Veda.

"I was in the treehouse," Lucia said.

"*The* treehouse, the Taj Ma-treehouse?" Simone asked.

"Yes, that's the one," Lucia said. "It's a great place to clear your mind, up there in the treetop. And the sunrise viewing can't be beat."

"Huh," Simone said. "Wait, did you know she was up there, Veda?"

"I didn't at first," Veda said. "But I started noticing the light was on at night. My husband was traveling, so I asked my brother-in-law Garrett to check it out. He was the one who found Lucia."

"But you didn't ever tell Lucia's mom?" I asked Veda.

"I begged Garrett and Veda to keep my secret," Lucia said. "I let Veda tell Mama, and the police, that I was safe."

"So, what's this event all about?" Lucia asked. "George told me I could find you here. I see meditation cushions and people walking with closed eyes. Did they drink your tea, Veda?"

"They did, in fact, drink my tea," Veda said. "We are bringing mindfulness practice to our community."

"Well, that's nice," Lucia said. "But did you know it's 6:30 a.m.?"

"It's a marathon of sorts," Simone said. "Now, would you please get a shower and give us a hand?"

"Lucia, your mom is in the other room praying," Veda said.

"Still?" Simone asked, eyebrows raised.

"Yes, let's go see her," Veda said.

Simone and I followed them.

"Mama?" Lucia said.

Lucia's mom turned from her kneeling position.

"Lucia, *mija*!" Lucia's mom said, jumping up.

Lucia rushed to her.

"Mama, I'm back," she said, hugging her. "*Estoy bien*."

We left Lucia and her mom alone to talk.

The day progressed in shifts of mindfulness, eating and resting. Visitors came and went. Kids napped and returned.

Week 5: Tools to Process Difficult Emotions

At 6 p.m., Veda's neighbor rang the doorbell.

"Could you give me a hand?" she asked me, wearing a long purple dress and matching turban. "My husband's coming with the main course, but I could use some help carrying in the sides and desserts."

We set up the main hall with a spread of tamales, rice, tea and benny cakes.

A loud rumble filled the room. Then stopped.

"What on earth was that?" Simone asked, marching to the front door.

As she opened up the front door, fifteen leather-clad men stood on the porch.

"I heard there's a fundraiser for Lucia, so I brought my Harley crew," Garrett said, his helmet in hand. "We're in for $300 each. Where do you want us?"

Simone hugged Garrett, a little longer than I expected.

"The event is wrapping up, but dinner is being served," Simone said. "If you'd like to join me … us."

Behind the Harley crew stood my father, Pat and our twins. The girls ran to find Adriana and Simone's kids. I gave Dad a hug, and he left to say hi to Lucia. Pat gave me a big hug and kissed my forehead.

"Guess Pat doesn't mind your short hair, after all," Simone whispered to me.

Veda guided us through experiencing the wonderfully delicious meal with our six senses.

We chimed in with our feedback.

Sight: I said, "I enjoy how the plethora of white sesame seeds look on the benny cakes."

Smell: Simone said, "The tea smells coconutty, like the oolong we enjoyed a few weeks ago."

Touch: Garrett said, "The banana wrap around the tamales feels slick and fibrous."

Taste: Lucia said, "My taste buds are a bit dull, but the acidic tomato flavor is still coming through."

Hear: Pat said, "I hear our tea cups clinking."

Mind: Veda said, "I notice how I feel intense joy and blissful memories as I eat this food."

After we cleaned up, Veda gave Lucia a Veda hug. Simone and I both took our turn.

"Now, don't go running off again," Simone said. "That treehouse door doesn't have a lock, you know."

"Actually, it does," Lucia said.

"You've *got* to be kidding me," Simone said. "Veda, you're going to have a whole brood of squatters before long. What should I tell the mailman my address is?"

"You girls are always good for a laugh," Veda said. "I'll see you next weekend for our silent retreat. I emailed you the address. It's a little south of here, at my family's vacation home. You may want to carpool.

"Like the name suggests, you'll be invited to stay quiet all day. I'll bring extra props and guide us through a few practices. We'll finish the day with a dinner. Lucia has offered to bring the main dish. If you three could coordinate the sides, I'll take care of the rest.

"Please leave your cell phones in the car," Veda said. "We might be shocked how beautifully quiet the woods can be without technology."

Chapter 8
Week 6: Day of Silence

In silence and in meditation on the eternal truths, I hear the voice of God which excites our hearts to greater love.

—C.S. Lewis

Simone was honking the horn as I pulled on my tennis shoes. Lucia waved from the back seat.

"Pat, I'm heading out," I said, giving him a peck on the lips. "I'll see you after dinner. The lasagna is in the fridge. Three hundred fifty degrees for fifty minutes or until it's bubbling."

I turned the doorknob and cracked open the door.

"Hey," he said, grabbing my left hand. "I hope you have a great day with your friends. This class seems good for you. You're more relaxed, happy and attentive."

He pulled me in for a big kiss.

Simone honked again, three times. When I opened the door, Simone was making a kissy face toward the window and Lucia was smiling and shaking her head.

I hopped in the passenger seat and slung my bag behind my seat.

"Well, someone is feeling frisky early in the morning," Simone said. "Looks like ol' Pat likes what he sees."

"He did say that I seem more relaxed and attentive," I said.

"Oh, did he now?" Simone said. "Sounds like he's saying he finally woke up to realize you're awfully pretty and he's glad you're his lady."

"Oh, Simone, you're something else," I said. "But, I think we'll go with what you said."

"It's supposed to be a day of silence," Simone said, putting the vehicle into gear. "But I can't get Lucia to quit yapping. Must be the perky yellow dress she's wearing. And her sassy new haircut."

"Is that my cue to tell you what's been going on since the fundraiser you so graciously hosted for me?" Lucia asked.

"Well, it sure as heck isn't to ask you how you plan to redecorate the Taj-Ma treehouse," Simone said.

"I did have an idea for some new drapes … ," Lucia said with a chuckle.

"Since I saw you last weekend, I sat down with Mama, Papa and Adriana," Lucia said. "We fully explained my condition to Adriana. She took the news pretty well, especially since we're working to raise money to offset my time away from work for treatment."

"And your mom," I said. "How's she taking it?"

"She is incredibly grateful for the Meditation-a-Thon you two and Veda put on for me," she said. "That seemed to relax her a bit, just knowing that I have dear friends looking out for me."

"And what about you, Lucia?" I asked. "How are you holding up? Or, as Veda would ask, 'What's been coming up for you?'"

"A lot has been coming up for me, as you can imagine," she said. "I've experienced feelings of grief. Concern for my parents and Adriana. Uncertainty about my future. Sometimes I feel angry, wondering why this is happening to me. I'm only 29 years old and have so much I want to accomplish and experience, places I want to see."

"I hear you, Lucia," I said. "And I appreciate your honesty."

"And what about you, missy?" Simone asked, looking sideways at me.

"Things are starting to improve between me and Pat," I said.

"I noticed," Simone said, raising her eyebrows up and down.

"I'm still not sure about my company's name," I said. "But I'm really enjoying the writing I'm doing for my new client."

"How are your kids?" Lucia asked, yawning. "Adriana would love a play date soon."

"My girls are doing well, enjoying their gymnastics, soccer and swimming clubs," I said. "Yes, let's get a play date on the books soon."

"And Pat's job, has it slowed down?" Lucia asked.

"No, but we're handling our family responsibilities more like a team," I said. "Speaking of family, I do have some news."

"Do tell," Simone said.

"You know that nausea I've been having?" I asked.

"I do recall some queasy looks over the last few weeks," Lucia said. "I know what nausea looks like now."

"Well, we're expecting Baby McNamara number three!"

Simone slammed on the brakes and pulled over on the highway.

"Shut the front door," Simone said. "Are you kidding me?"

"Nope, not kidding you," I replied.

"When are you due?" Lucia asked.

"Sometime around Christmas," I said.

"Congratulations, sweetie," Simone said, hugging me. "Guess you got that adventure you've been wanting, Agent Double-O Seven. Only difference is that this one doesn't include wearing sexy dresses in an exotic location."

"How are you feeling now?" Lucia asked.

"Like I have the flu," I said.

"That ought to make a really fun day of silence," Simone said, merging back onto the road. "Can't say I envy you that one bit. Don't you and Lucia go tag-team puking in my car."

Before long, we pulled up a long private gravel road. A large limestone house popped up over the fern-laden hills.

"Whoa, is that the cabin?" I asked. "I thought we'd be in a small, rustic house."

"This family sure has a funny way of naming its dwellings," Simone said. "I'd call this a woodland castle."

Veda greeted us at the front door with a bow.

"Welcome," she said. "Please follow me."

She led us past the kitchen and family room to a room nestled in the middle of the home. A fire was blazing in the wood-burning fireplace. Veda's mat and kneeling bench were set up at the far end of the room.

"You may set up your mats here," she said. "I'll give you a tour of the home, as you're invited to spread out to practice mindful movement and eating."

We followed her upstairs to the master suite with cathedral-like windows.

"I feel like I'm in a treehouse," Lucia said.

"Right at home then, I guess," Simone said with a wink.

A small sunroom tucked around the corner looked like a great place to sit.

Down the hallway was another bedroom, a super quiet spot I'd like to snag at some point in the day.

Back in the meditation room, Veda began our day with some reminders.

"Welcome to our day of silence," she said. "It's a day not only of verbal silence, but of silence of the eyes, meaning we keep our eyes to ourselves. We'll be focused inwardly in our practice today. If you haven't already, please turn off all phones, watches and other devices. I'd strongly recommend these are left in the car."

My phone was in Simone's car.

I wonder if Pat got the girls to practice this morning. Maybe he left me a text.

"Let's begin with a sitting practice," Veda said. "Remember it's your practice today, so please take care of your needs quietly throughout our time together."

I set up my kneeling position on my bolster. Simone sat cross-legged. Veda sat on her kneeling stool and Lucia on a chair.

Ding.

I should've peed before I sat down. I bet we'll be here for forty-five minutes or so. I'll likely need to take care of this before I hear the bell ding three times. It was so fun to tell Simone and Lucia about my pregnancy. Ugh, I'm feeling a wave of nausea pass through me. OK, we are sitting. Seeing thoughts pass by like clouds. A passing cloud—that could be my new mantra. Look at me using woo-woo terms. I see the pregnancy thoughts bubble. Pat bubble. He's so cute, and I appreciate him taking care of the girls today. I wonder if Angelina will land her cartwheel today? I hope Pat texts me a cartwheel video. Thinking.

I tapped my leg and snuck a look at my friends. Their eyes were closed.

What a peaceful moment. I haven't experienced quiet like this in years. Or ever. Now I just need to quiet down my thinking. Observe it quietly and slowly. I'm breathing in and feel my belly expanding. Soon, that's the size it's going to be all the time. I'm breathing out and feel my breath cross my lips and my belly deflating.

Ding, ding, ding.

"Please join me on the deck as we practice being present with our six senses," Veda said. "Be sure to bring along your journals."

Once outside, we gathered in a half-circle facing the woods. Veda handed us each a Honeycrisp apple.

Week 6: Day of Silence

"Notice what you see," Veda said. "Really look at the apple in your hands. Feel free to note your observations in your notebook throughout the exercise or at the end."

I saw that it was pinkish-red and splotched with yellow. The stem looked healthy, slightly thicker at the top. I found some light brown dots and stripes. I jotted down my observations in my purple journal.

"What do you hear when you touch the apple?" Veda asked.

I heard a waxy *shhh*, a little squeak. The stem grunted a bit when I twisted it. And the brown bottom tuft—what was that thing called? I never thought to name that. I heard a slight *huhh* when I touched that.

"What do you feel?" Veda asked. "Perhaps the stalk at the top or the calyx at the bottom?"

Ah, the calyx.

I felt a waxy outer skin. I closed my eyes and felt some bumps and dents. The apple felt firm, like it would be a crunchy one, my favorite.

"Turning our attention to smell," Veda said. "Notice the scent of the apple."

I smell a sweet-sour grassy scent. I can't wait to bite this apple. Hopefully tasting is next.

"Now, the moment you may've been waiting for ... taste," Veda said. "When you're ready, you are invited to take a bite of the apple, noticing what you see, hear, taste, smell and feel."

Crunch, crunch, crunch.

Honeycrisps are the best. What a fabulous ka-chunk crunch. *What a firm texture it has. I see a light beige-yellow inside, the size of a golf ball, where I've taken a bite. The flavor is sweet with the slightest sour undertones.*

"Take a few moments to finish writing your sensations, including your thoughts about the apple, which may have come up along the way."

As we put down our pens, I looked up to see Veda rising from her seat.

Ding, ding, ding.

"Please join me on the far side of the deck for mindful walking," she said. "I will sound the bell when our walking practice has concluded."

In silence, we spread out on the deck, with plenty of space to wander with our eyes open or closed.

Ding.

As I began walking, I realized that walking was hard for me.

I always run from one thing to the next—client meetings, school pick-ups, errands, extracurricular activities. And, I'm a runner, and have been since high school. Paying attention to my walking sounds like a foreign concept. OK, I'm noticing some resistance and see that I'm on the other side of the deck while the other gals are only half-way across. I'd better slow down. How do I do this again? Right, close my eyes. Feel my feet against the ground. Then my toes. Notice how my legs move and hips shift, and I move my legs. And wobble a bit. My feet rock as they support the shift of setting down the opposite leg. My arms move a bit, too.

When I run, I try to time my breathing to my steps. Let's try that. Lift my right foot, inhaling. Set right foot down as I exhale. Now lift my left foot and inhale. Then set my left foot down as I exhale.

Week 6: Day of Silence

After several trips back and forth on the deck, I felt in the zone.

Ding, ding, ding.

We joined Veda back in the half-circle.

"Silence can be challenging to find," Veda said. "I invite you to soak it in and write or draw about silence in your journals. You may notice your senses around silence. You might note how you feel silence and how you feel about it. Remember to breathe deeply."

Ding.

I placed my journal on my lap and closed my eyes. I heard a woodpecker in the distance. A cardinal chirping. The *tink-tank* of the creek below. But not a word was spoken.

I wonder how Lucia managed to stay alone that week in the treehouse. What did she experience in the silence? And what did she learn? In silence, I notice discomfort. I keep patting my back pocket, afraid I've lost my phone or missed a message. I feel tension in my shoulders. I'll take a deep breath.

In silence I feel a deep understanding that it's not all up to me. I don't have to fight what is going on around me. Or inside me.

I began writing: *Silence is an invitation. An invitation to sit inside our own home, our internal temple, and know. To open up to what is. To stop struggling and accept. Perhaps I need to accept the season of life that I'm in, one of significant activity, full of ball games and baby dolls, Play-Doh and popsicles. It won't always be this way. I won't always have my girls at home. Or this baby in my belly. The best gift I can give my children is the real me, fully present and full of life and love.*

In silence, I know that being a working parent is challenging with long days and little gratitude. I let myself breathe to connect with who I am, the real me that I often neglect. I can invest in me and invest in my family. I sit with the discomfort of silence. The not-knowing of silence. The pause of silence.

Ding, ding, ding.

"Please join me inside for some mindful movement," Veda said. "Lucia, please take it easy and rest if you feel tired at any point."

On my mat, I saw Veda add a couple more logs to the fire. She returned to her mat, standing with her eyes closed. The heat of the stove warmed my legs.

Ding.

With the fire roaring, we began by grounding our feet in mountain pose, standing straight with feet shoulder-width apart. We felt the four corners of our feet.

"Lift your arms to the sky," Veda said. "Now into two worlds. Arms in a T, now curling into your shoulders."

A cat-cow movement led us to downward dog and back to mountain pose.

"Join me in child's pose."

Our child's pose stretch transitioned into a short sitting meditation.

We ended in Shavasana, or corpse pose. I heard Lucia snoring a bit.

Ding, ding, ding.

"I invite you to partake in a silent lunch," Veda said. "Lucia will place the food she prepared on the table shortly. You are free to eat there or anywhere on the property. We will have about a forty-five-minute lunch break. Remember to take your time and use your senses to eat mindfully."

Week 6: Day of Silence

I filled my plate with two tacos and some fruit. I sat in the super quiet bedroom to eat.

Wow, the tacos are loaded with flavor—paprika, cilantro, lime, and queso blanco. They're warm and soft, little stuffed blankets.

I wolfed down the first taco, then ate my pineapple slowly, noticing the pulpy strings catching in my teeth. I ate the second taco more slowly. I wondered where the other women chose to eat. At home I often eat alone while the girls are at school and Pat is at work. I kept feeling the itch to check my phone.

I can't remember when today's retreat is over. I need to check my email from Veda. What time am I meeting the family for dinner? And did we decide on a location? I feel awkward not looking at my phone. Like part of my brain is sitting inside Simone's shiny SUV. I could go check it since no one else is out here.

I breathed through the temptation to grab my phone, choosing instead to walk to the kitchen to clean my dishes. The house felt empty.

I heard a *ding* from the fireplace room and headed back to my mat.

"Please join me outside for a nature walk," Veda said. "Lucia, you may use this time to sit outdoors, if that serves you."

Lucia shook her head and followed us to the trailhead.

At the trailhead, Veda instructed us to spread out and find one natural item on the trail to bring back. We'd circle up again on the deck after we'd finished the trail. We were taking our walking meditation to another level by walking on a trail. We'd keep our eyes open, of course, but feel our feet and movements, touch leaves and branches.

Simone went first down the trail, then I began, Lucia followed at a distance, followed by Veda.

I felt cocooned by the moist trail and tree canopy shading us. A few downed trees created trail borders. I heard the crack of twigs beneath my feet. I smelled damp leaves and loamy mud. A gray squirrel shook a tree up ahead. Mesmerized by the quiet beauty surrounding me, I forgot to pick up a natural item. Back at the trailhead, I saw a small white pebble nestled in a patch of moss. Moss is magical in my world. I scooped up a patch of the moss with the pebble and brought it to the deck to meet the other women.

I looked back to show my moss-covered pebble to Lucia, but no one was behind me.

"Lucia," I whispered, as I retraced my steps.

Then louder: "Lucia!"

I looked down the ravine. A swath of bright yellow fabric caught my eye.

"Simone! Veda!" I yelled as I managed my way down the ravine.

I turned Lucia over gently, revealing what she held in her hand: an opaque leaf with a small brown leaf pressed into it like natural paper.

"Lucia, are you OK?" I asked. "Can you hear me?"

Simone seemed to appear out of nowhere. She stuffed her piece of bark with mint-colored growth in her back pocket. She picked up Lucia in her arms and carried her up the ravine, her left arm around Lucia's waist and Lucia's legs draping over Simone's right arm. Lucia hugged Simone's neck loosely, and her head bobbed a bit. She winced as Simone had to lean to make it up the incline.

Lucia's gotten very thin—wow. I'm not sure she's even a hundred pounds.

Back in the house, Veda prepared a bed for Lucia.

At her bedside, Veda soothed Lucia.

"It is time," Veda said to Lucia. Veda looked up at us.

I stopped breathing.

"I'm not quite ready," Lucia said.

Silently, Veda handed us our journals and pens.

"Let's give Lucia some time to rest," Veda said. "I invite you to check in with yourself. Please take ten minutes to write or draw about the natural item you brought back," she said.

She rang the bell to start our creation practice.

How on earth am I supposed to write at this moment? One of my best friends is lying on a bed in a cabin one hour from home. I think she's dying. I'm scared, and I'm supposed to write. Fine … It's a white pebble with hairy moss. There. Now I can try to come up with a plan to help Lucia.

Veda held a white mushroom that filled the palm of her hand. It looked bumpy like frog skin.

I need to call Pat. He'll know what to do.

Ding, ding, ding.

"Please join us by Lucia's bedside," Veda said.

Veda sat next to Lucia, holding her hand. She looked at me then Simone.

"I need to tell you two something," Lucia said. "Something I've hidden from you for many years."

Veda pulled up some chairs for us to sit.

"As you know, when I was in college, I traveled with my fiancé to Sierra Leone. With my engineering and his accounting skills, we helped lead a big building team with Meghan's father. On the last night of the trip, we decided we couldn't wait any longer to be married. We asked Meghan's dad to marry us. With Veda's help, we held a private mountaintop ceremony.

"That night, I slept with my husband for the first time. In the morning, I awoke so happy. I kissed him, but he didn't respond. He was cold and wouldn't wake."

Veda handed Lucia a tissue.

"My beloved Pedro, officially named Peter Hazeldine, died that night, our wedding night," Lucia said. "He had an undetected heart defect, and apparently our mountaintop wedding was too much for his weak heart."

Heart defect. Married to Lucia. Died. Wait, Hazeldine is Veda's last name.

"My father was distraught that I didn't marry in the church," Lucia said. "And Meghan's father felt so guilty that he didn't notice anything wrong with Pedro. He promised never to tell we were married to anyone besides my and Pedro's families."

"But a few weeks after Pedro's funeral, I began swelling," Lucia said. "I moved away to the other side of the country. Because I was pregnant."

She looked from me to Simone.

"Adriana is my daughter. Not my sister's."

As if she heard the questions racing through my mind, she responded.

"I kept this secret for family honor," Lucia said. "I wasn't married in the church, and it seemed more appropriate for Adriana to be raised by my sister and her husband. Since they live next door to my parents and me, it worked out."

"It's a lot to take in," Veda said. "I know it's a day of silence, but if you'd like to take a few moments to speak, I welcome it."

"Does Adriana know?" I asked.

"Not yet," Lucia said. "I wanted to give her time to process my cancer news first."

I felt a ball of confusing energy rising in me. Shock, sadness, anger, betrayal.

How could Lucia keep something this huge from me? How could I not have known? Doesn't she trust me?

"Remember when I moved to my aunt's house in California for that internship right after the mission trip?" Lucia said.

"We all knew you were struggling after Pedro died," I said. "I understood why you wanted to move away."

"True," Lucia said. "And the internship was real, but it also helped me cover up my pregnancy and Adriana's birth."

"I do recall you ghosting me for the better part of a year," Simone said. "It was a bit of a Mystery of the Missing Maiden situation."

Veda pulled out their wedding photo. Light radiated behind them in the mountain cleft. Passing clouds suspended in time.

"And here are the mustard bushes," Veda said, pulling out another photo. "Planted by Lucia and Peter that joyful, yet tragic night. They have grown nearly twenty feet tall and are a blessing to the people in Sierra Leone."

Ah ha, the empty glass orbs—one on Lucia's wrist, the other tied to the tree! The haunting pine tree. Planted for Pedro, Lucia's husband and Veda's nephew—Peter, as she knew him.

Silence hung in the air. Simone rubbed her own shoulder. I couldn't look any of them in the eye.

"For once in my life, I'm not sure what to say," Simone said.

"Thank you for sharing all this, Lucia," I said. "I feel sad knowing you've held this in for all these years. What a load to carry. I'm sure I'll have a million questions later, but those can wait."

Lucia grabbed my hand.

"I feel so free with all of this off my chest," she said. "Like Frank said, 'Sometimes things don't turn out like we hope.' But I choose to be hopeful anyway."

"Who is Frank?" Veda asked.

"My chemo buddy."

"And apparently an admirer of yours," I said. "He went on and on about you and your aura and lost chances to win your heart."

"Oh my, I haven't thought of Frank in many years," Veda said. "We were quite close for much of my formative years and into college. I'm sad to hear he's in chemo. How is his treatment coming along?"

Week 6: Day of Silence

"Not well," Lucia said. "His doctor has given him three months to live."

Veda's eyes glistened.

"I ..." she said, her voice catching. "I notice tears in my eyes, blurred vision, a tight throat and a weight in the center of my chest that I would describe as sadness."

Lucia reached into her pocket and pulled out the two brown heart-shaped stones.

"He told me I could keep these, to remember him, to remember that even if things don't always turn out like we hope, sometimes a new path we'd never considered might open up for us. But that's only if we're willing to let go of the life we imagined and embrace the one we have."

"Beautifully said," Veda said, a tear slipping down her cheek.

Lucia shifted in bed.

"My right leg really hurts," Lucia said. "I think I injured it."

"Lucia, your parents are on their way," Veda said. "Why don't you rest while Meghan, Simone and I finish the day."

"No," Lucia said, sitting up with a struggle. "I will finish today's practices. I'm tired, but I will survive."

Veda nodded.

We helped Lucia limp to the fireplace room.

Veda helped Lucia get comfortable in a chair for a sitting meditation. The rest of us began with mindful walking back and forth on our mats. Veda sounded the bell, and I practiced breathing in as I lifted my foot and breathing out as I gently placed my foot on the ground. As I felt the end of the mat, I turned slowly and breathed in and out three times, then began walking across the mat again.

I saw Simone and Veda walking quietly with their eyes closed.

What a peaceful vision. It doesn't take much room to practice mindfulness. I may set up a small space at home to dedicate to my practice.

Veda sounded the bell three times to end our walking meditation.

"We'll conclude our mindfulness practice with sitting, then circle up afterward in this room for a discussion," Veda said. "You may sit here or somewhere else in the house."

Ding.

I took my cushion up to the nook off the master suite upstairs. I saw Simone headed to the second bedroom at the end of the hall. Lucia and Veda stayed by the fireplace.

Once settled on my cushion, I worked to focus on my breath, slowly breathing in and out.

Lucia is Adriana's mom. Lucia is a mom. How did I never suspect this? Why didn't Lucia ever tell me? Lucia's part of Veda's family. This is too much to take in. Thinking. I'm thirsty. I hope we have some tea. I wonder what time it is. Breathe in. My leg feels like it's going numb.

I adjusted on my cushion.

I need to pee again. Breathing in. This has been a dramatic day of peace and joy, fear and worry. Breathing out. My thoughts feel more manageable, like slowly moving clouds, not zooming racecars.

Ding, ding, ding.

Week 6: Day of Silence

When I returned to the gathering room, I placed a couple more logs on the fire. We circled up and looked at each other's eyes for the first time since we began.

"Thank you for your vulnerability today," Veda said. "I'd love to hear what came up for you."

"I felt an itch to check my phone nearly all day," I said. "But felt that urge slowly start to ease up near the end."

"I wanted to take pictures with my phone at the beginning," Simone said. "The views here are stunning."

"I feel deeply relieved to share what I've held in for so many years," Lucia said. "I felt the weight of my family's concern and sadness, but also the glimmer of hope we have for my treatments."

"That apple was off the hook," Simone said. "Who knew an apple could taste so good?"

"Agreed," I said.

"I kept thinking about Meghan's news," Simone said.

"What might that be, if you're willing to share?" Veda asked.

"I'm expecting," I said.

"Congratulations, Meghan," Veda said. "How are you feeling?"

"Rather nauseated," I said. "Sometimes being so in touch with sensations can be quite uncomfortable."

"Amen to that," Lucia said.

"Meghan, have you spoken with your doctor about mindful movement and our other practices since learning you're pregnant?" Veda asked.

"Yes," I said. "She gave me the green light."

"Marvelous. One thing you may notice is that today's practice or the practice we've engaged in over the last several weeks may produce results long after today," Veda said. "Silence and mindfulness can be powerful tools for insight."

"Thank you for this course, Veda," Lucia said.

"Many thanks, Veda," I said. "What would you recommend we do next?"

"Besides take Lucia to the hospital *tout de suite*?" Simone said.

"I will tend to Lucia," Veda said. "Her mother and father are on the way."

"OK," Simone said, like a warning.

"I'll leave you with a guide to our lessons," she said. "As well as a list of resources for local weekly meditations and daily practice support. Remember to be GLOWY, my friends."

She lifted her hands in prayer position.

"As for, 'What do we do next?'" Veda said. "Let's have some tea!"

Chapter 9
Six Months Later

Our own life has to be our message.
—Thich Nhat Hanh

"Decaf cappuccino," announced the bohemian barista, who donned a Santa Claus hat. My beach-ball-sized belly bumped the tinsel-and-light-laden counter as I grabbed my mug. I sniffed its deep, earthy aroma with a twinge of angst.

Decaf cappuccino. Sounds like a compound curse word. I wonder if it's possible to die of caffeine withdrawal. Maybe. Then everyone could exclaim, "Decaf cappuccino!"

Back at the cafe table, I heard the door ring. The morning sun glittered through the opening.

"Simone!" I said, waving from the back corner.

In her high heels, tailored ruby dress, she and her huge beige purse maneuvered the crowded coffee shop.

"Hey, mama!" she said, hugging me and rubbing my belly. "Let me get some caffeine, and I'll be right back."

"Lucky," I said.

She smiled over her shoulder.

Another ding announced Lucia and Veda's entrance.

I waved and Simone flagged them to the ordering counter. Lucia was still using a cane, which she'd used since after the day she fell down the ravine. Luckily she didn't break her leg, but with a depressed immune system, recovery from a fall like that took time.

Back at the table, we sat quietly, smelling our drinks and taking slow, mindful sips.

"Sure you don't want a sip, Meghan?" Simone offered.

"I'll pass," I said. "My nausea is in full swing today. It's all I can do to keep this unleaded cappuccino down."

"I hear you, girlfriend," Lucia said. "That's rough."

Is it just me or does Lucia's skin look yellow? The whites of her eyes look yellow to me, too.

"Speaking of rough, how's chemo going, Lucia?" I asked. "Are you still planning to take a break?"

"Hold your clipboard, Detective Meg," Simone said. "First, we must have a toast. Lucia is alive!"

She raised her glass.

"To Lucia kicking cancer's butt!" Simone said.

"Cheers!" we said in unison.

We clinked mugs and drank. Lucia nearly dropped her mug, but saved it with just a little spill.

Six Months Later

"To answer your question, I've recently moved on to radiation, which is a daily treatment," she said. "I do have some spots on my liver, which is scary. But I have less pain right now."

"The liver spots worry me," I said. "But I'm grateful to hear you are in less pain."

"The cancer seems to be responding to radiation, so we're discussing a little break, just until after the holidays. And after the new year, I'll move to an oral medication that I can take at home. The cancer is still considered terminal, but we're working to extend what time I have left."

"And your relationship with Adriana is still going smoothly, since you've had the big talk?" Simone said. "You know, the one about you being her mom."

"When I told her, it felt like she already knew," Lucia said. "Like she inherited my mama's seventh sense of knowing everything. She just smiled and gave me a hug, a Veda hug."

Lucia pushed back her cuticles.

"But, since then we've had some awkward moments," she said. "Sometimes she's a bit distant. Just processing, I'm sure. I'm cherishing the official title of Mama, but worried about how to navigate our changing relationship."

"And your sister?" I asked. "How's she handling it?"

"She seems relieved," she said. "It was hard for her to keep the secret from Adriana all these years. Now it's all in the open, and we don't have to have hushed conversations anymore."

"What about you, Simone?" Lucia asked. "How's your new job going? Still getting along with your boss?"

"I can't believe how lucky I am," she said. "Who would've thought that me leading your fundraiser would've landed me a job helping disadvantaged youth via the university? That building still smells of palo santo from our fundraiser!"

"Congratulations on your new job, Simone," Veda said.

"They were impressed that we were able to raise just over $50 thousand for Lucia," Simone said. "Which is thanks in part to a last-minute $10 thousand donation from Lucia's work, a $10 thousand donation Garrett provided from Pedro's memorial fund … and a gift from an anonymous donor that will provide money each year to Lucia."

"Who was the anonymous donor?" I asked.

"Anonymous," Simone said, sipping her coffee. "OK, fine. You pulled it out of me. It was Frank. After he passed a few months ago, his estate went to Lucia since he didn't have any kids."

Veda took a long, quiet drink of tea.

"I'm sorry for your loss, Veda," I said. "Frank was quite fond of you."

"And I of him," Veda said. "He was a kind, generous soul who will be greatly missed."

A few moments of silence passed. Lucia took a deep breath in and out.

"And how is Garrett?" Lucia said, looking at Simone then Veda.

"I told you I can't resist a man on a motorcycle," Simone said, bopping her shoulders. "I love how Garrett takes me on long rides around town. He's also been helping me better manage my finances. Only one new purse a season, ladies. The sacrifices we make for love!"

"How wonderful," Veda said. "And what about you, Meghan?"

"I never told you, but I was considering an international client with lots of travel," I said. "But decided to stay close to home for now. I registered my business and chose the name McNamara Communications. I know it's not original, but people in the city know me and my husband. I thought I'd build on our family brand a bit."

"Congratulations, Meghan!" Simone said. "We need to celebrate."

She looked at my belly, then back at my face.

"After the baby is born," she said. "What are you having, anyway?"

"Drum roll, please," I said. "The McNamara family is having ... a baby boy!"

"Yay!" Simone said. "Boys are awesome. My son could use another boy around."

Simone reached into her purse and handed me a blue handbag.

"For you, Mama Meg," she said.

"What if I'd said it was a girl?" I asked.

She pulled out a pink handbag. I gave her a convicting look.

"What?" she said. "I plan to return it!"

"What about your writing, Meghan?" Veda asked. "Have you decided on the MFA?"

"I'm keeping in touch with your husband," I said. "I may apply to start next year, after the baby's born."

"Which is any day now!" Simone said, looking at my belly.

"And you, Veda," I said. "What's your world like these days?"

"I'm slowing down a bit, girls," she said. "As I sit, I feel more tired. My mother has been sick, and my son, who's grown now, is moving back from Portland. He's wanting to move back in with me and my husband. I'm open to helping him out while he tries to find a new job, but my husband wants our son to find his own way. It's causing a little tension at home."

"I'll be presenting our class findings to the university soon," Veda said. "So it's a good time to discuss it with you. Let's start with what you learned through the course and what you've been practicing since we last met."

"I can sit better with the uncertainty of life," Lucia said. "I find that where I'm most in the mindfulness zone is when I'm making food and doing the body scan. Cooking food provides a meaningful connection between my mind and body. And the body scan helps me tend to my sick body and be less scared by befriending my body. I've been sitting with my Mama, Papa and Adriana. It's a beautiful, human connection that seems to calm us as we face my sickness together."

"I'm trying to accept that I don't know the answers to everything, and that's OK," Simone said. "I've been walking mindfully over my lunch break. I usually keep my eyes open if I walk outdoors, but if I'm in my office, I'll close the door and practice walking back and forth across my office. It helps me stay in my body. I can get carried away throughout the day, but the walking helps me come back to myself, feel my feet on the ground, reconnect with my rhythmic breath. I'll also sing mindfully, feeling my vocal cords, meditating on the words and notes, letting the notes hum through my body."

"I'm learning to be present even when the world is spinning in chaos," I said. "Of course, I can't do that every moment of my life. But, practicing daily, even for five minutes, is a huge help in cultivating this ability. I've carved out a corner of a room in my house for sitting, writing and movement, my favorite mindfulness practices. When I write, I'll often focus deeply on one thing—perhaps a piece of fruit from my kitchen or a drawing from one of my girls. It's still hard not to hop on my phone to check social media or plan the day or prep dinner. But, when I'm fully present for this quiet time, then I'm more present for my writing. It's very therapeutic and calming. I feel connected with myself in an authentic, meaningful way. It's like my writing is saying, 'I see you, Meghan.'"

"Beautiful," Veda said. "I've noticed that my kneeling position has gotten uncomfortable, so I've switched to a seated position, a cushion or just a firm chair. I'm learning to have compassion for myself and my aging body."

"Speaking of struggles," Lucia said. "I'm struggling to focus. With treatments and my parents, my job and official motherhood, I feel a bit overwhelmed. Adriana has been so sweet. She's selling her artwork to raise money for our family. Simone has been very gracious to display and sell Adriana's paintings and drawings at the university. However, when Adriana's not working on her artwork, she's on her phone and tablet constantly. It feels like she's in a bit of denial and deep in the world of escape."

"Well, you don't want her to have to get a pet lynx like Queen Alba to learn her lesson," Simone said. "My kids are moving in that direction with technology. And talking back, unmindful actions and speech."

"My girls are struggling with technology and screen time, too," I said. "We have limits, but it feels like they're addicted and struggle with boredom. Any tips for imparting our mindfulness knowledge to our children, Veda?"

She smiled broadly.

"Dear ones, I think you've given me a great idea for my next course!"

With a deep bow, she exited the coffee shop.

Ding.

An Invitation
Download Your Free Six-Week Mindfulness Guide!

To say thank you, and help you on your own wellness journey, I've developed a six-week mindfulness guide—and you can download it for FREE! In this guide I've outlined the basic principles included in *The Chaos Antidote: A Fable About Mindfulness.*

What you'll get:

- The GLOWY daily reflection practice
- Mindful exercises that mirror the book's weekly lessons
- Engaging homework assignments that help you develop your own mindfulness practice

Visit **aimeemorgan.com/chaosantidote** to claim your FREE copy today!

APPENDIX A
Reading List

I read the following books prior to and during the writing of my book. They've provided deep life knowledge for me and inspiration for my mindful pursuits:

Anam Cara: A Book of Celtic Wisdom by John O'Donohue

The Artist's Way by Julia Cameron

The Art of Power by Thich Nhat Hanh, and many other books by Thich Nhat Hanh

Braving the Wilderness by Brené Brown

Cultivate by Lara Casey

Dare to Lead by Brené Brown

Daring Greatly by Brené Brown

Emotional Agility by Susan David

The Gifts of Imperfection by Brené Brown

Girl, Wash Your Face by Rachel Hollis

The Hero's Journey: Joseph Campbell on His Life and Work by Joseph Campbell

The Monk Who Sold His Ferrari by Robin S. Sharma

The Power of TED* (The Empowerment Dynamic) by David Emerald

Several books by Jon Kabat-Zinn and Pema Chödrön

Appendix B
Recipe: Super Vegetable Soup

In Chapter 4 (Awakening the Senses), the women prepare Super Vegetable Soup in silence. They chop, smell and taste as they prepare this soup, filled with fresh vegetables and a tasty broth. Veda reminds them that just as the broth softens the vegetables, our mindful breath softens our mind so it is supple to experience life. I invite you to prepare the Super Vegetable Soup in silence, using all your senses to experience the food and appreciate the cooking process.

Yields: approximately 8-10 servings

Prep time: 45 minutes

Ingredients

Sauté

2 Tbsp olive oil

1 medium yellow onion, chopped

2 cups carrots, peeled and chopped (about 4-5 carrots)

1 ¼ cups celery, chopped (about 3 stalks)

4 cloves fresh garlic, minced

Slow cooker

32-oz. low-sodium vegetable broth

5-oz. bottle of Tad McBride Sauces Samurai Sauce*

3 cups diced potatoes, peeled and ½-inch thick (about 4 or 5 medium potatoes)

Kernels from 2 cobs of corn (or 1 can, drained or about 1 ½ cups frozen)

1 ½ cups (½ lb.) fresh green beans, trimmed and cut in thirds (or 1 can drained)

⅛ tsp paprika

¼ tsp crushed red pepper (optional)

Salt and pepper to taste

Optional: 2 lbs. uncooked chicken breast or roast beef (shred before serving)

Directions

1. Heat olive oil in a large pot over medium-high heat.
2. Add onion, carrots and celery. Sauté 4 minutes. Add garlic and sauté 30 seconds more.
3. Transfer the onion mixture to the slow cooker.
4. Add broth, Tad McBride Sauces Samurai Sauce, potatoes, corn and green beans. Stir well.
5. Add paprika and crushed red pepper (optional). Salt and pepper to taste.
6. Mix thoroughly in slow cooker.
7. Add enough water to cover all the vegetables.
8. Optional: Add uncooked chicken or roast beef (if added, ensure all meat and vegetables are covered by the liquid).
9. Turn slow cooker on high for 4-6 hours or low for 8-10 hours.

*Tad McBride Sauces Samurai Sauce is available online at tadmcbridesauces.com and in select retail stores.

Additional Recipes

Visit aimeemorgan.com for the following recipes:

- Posh Roast
- Spicy Chicken Ka-bomb Kabobs
- Tropical Shrimp Ka-bomb Kabobs
- Super Vegetable Soup (Quick version)
- And more!

Appendix C
GLOWY Daily Reflection Practice (2–3 minutes)

GLOWY is an acronym you can use in your daily practice.

- **G** stands for "grateful." You can identify things that are a blessing.
- **L** is for "lift up," for the things that need attention/prayer.
- **O** is for "observe," to remind you to pay attention to what you notice in your mind, body and soul.
- **W** stands for "wholesome intention," what you intend for yourself and your day.
- **Y** is for "you are," the beginning of positive statements about yourself.

The GLOWY Daily Reflection Practice

Take three deep breaths in and out. Then connect with yourself by reflecting on the following:

I am **G**rateful for _____.

I **L**ift up _____.

I **O**bserve _____.

My **W**holesome intention is _____.

You are _____.

Take three deep breaths in and out.

Acknowledgments

A special thank you to my tribe who generously supported me in the multi-layer development of this book:

- My husband, Jeff, for his encouragement, reading, editing and support throughout the process of writing this book. Thank you for being an amazing father to our kids. We love you, babe!
- Alyssa Chase, a brilliant poet and cherished friend/mentor who encouraged me to follow my passion for writing and creating essentially from the moment we met.
- Erin Slater, my coach, who encouraged and supported me in every step of this journey.
- My insightful and talented editor, Nancy Pile, who helped me refine my manuscript into its final form.
- Gary Williams, my writing coach, who served as a fount of encouragement and information.
- Emily Wiland, fellow MFA candidate, who reviewed large sections of my initial manuscript, offering insightful edits and encouragement.
- David Shields, prolific author, who provided excellent feedback on a portion of my manuscript.
- Enola, a lifelong friend who provided encouragement on my book when I most needed it.

- My creative father, Tad McBride, for his support and love, as well as his help developing custom recipes for my book and website that feature his outstanding line of sauces. Check them out at tadmcbridesauces.com!
- My talented brother, Daniel McBride, who designed my book cover.
- My thorough and patient formatter, Pankaj Runthala, who helped bring my text to life.
- A heartfelt thank you to my beta readers:
    - Casey Bales, certified cancer researcher
    - Kristen Fuhs Wells
    - Andra Kramer
    - Sebastian Seibert
    - Dominique Weldon

A special thank you to Scott Sweet, Licensed Clinical Social Worker (LCSW) and Licensed Clinical Addictions Counselor (LCAC), who led the Mindfulness-Based Stress Reduction (MBSR) course I completed, and served as a beta reader.

About the Author

Aimee Morgan is the owner of Good Aim Communications—goodaimcommunications.com—a WBE-certified strategic marketing communications company that specializes in website development, content creation and digital marketing. She's spent over 15 years in the marketing field honing her craft.

Her successful work includes an Emmy-award-winning video ad series and a Public Relations Society of America Pinnacle Award for the Spirit & Place Festival marketing campaign.

Aimee discovered the path to mindfulness the way many people do—by facing hard times. Raised in Spiceland, Indiana, and married at 20 while an undergraduate, Aimee built her life around her marriage, faith and career. However, a crisis of faith, career setbacks and relational struggles left her feeling powerless and adrift. After a life-threatening miscarriage, Aimee started to realize how unhappy she'd become. Her life was in chaos.

Aimee began to train both her mind and body through the practice of mindfulness. She completed the Mindfulness-Based Stress Reduction course developed by Jon Kabat-Zinn, where she learned how to accept discomfort instead of reacting to it—and how to be grateful and let joy sink in. She spent years studying, practicing and discussing the value of mindfulness, self-care and healthful ways of living, unearthing the transformative power of the present moment.

Aimee graduated cum laude from Butler University, where she earned bachelor's degrees in journalism and Spanish. She's currently pursuing a master of fine arts degree in creative writing. She lives in Indianapolis with her husband, Jeff, and their two young children. *The Chaos Antidote: A Fable About Mindfulness* is her first book. You can learn more about the author and her book at **aimeemorgan.com**.